I'M BORED!

First published 2003

Copyright © Suzy Barratt and Polly Beard, 2003
Illustrations copyright © Sam Holland, 2003

The moral right of the authors has been asserted
Bloomsbury Publishing Plc,
36 Soho Square, London W1D 3QY

A CIP catalogue record for this book
is available from the British Library

ISBN 0747563217
ISBN 13 9780747563211

Designed by Richard Horne

10 9 8 7 6 5

Printed and bound in Singapore by Tien Wah Press
www.bloomsbury.com/suzybarratt

ACKNOWLEDGEMENTS

We would like to thank:

Joss and Tom for everything.

Jane Turnbull for her belief in us.

Rosemary Davidson and everyone at
Bloomsbury for their support and guidance.

Sam for her beautiful drawings.

Granny Trish and Granny Lily for their
wonderful help with our kids.

And finally, Mum, Dad and Em for
teaching us how to play in the first place.

FOR

Joss and Elmo – SB

Tom, Ella and Jojo – PB

CONTENTS

INTRODUCTION 8

INTRODUCTION

When your children are bored and can't think of what to do next, it is often impossible to come up with an immediate and brilliant idea that will keep everyone happy – especially if your brain is otherwise engaged in cooking tea, making a phone call or negotiating a tricky one-way system. As busy mothers ourselves, we've often longed for a book that would give us ideas for what to play, how to play it and, most importantly, remind us how to enjoy playing it with our kids.

Inside are games we play with our children, some we used to play as children ourselves, and others that you may be familiar with but might have forgotten how to play. Treat it as you would a recipe book. Dip in and out of it when you need fresh ideas and inspiration. Some of the games are short and sweet. Others may last for days on end. There are ideas for toddlers on their own or a whole pack of pre-pubescent boys. Start your kids off with any of the games – you may find that they will grasp the idea quickly and play on their own or you may be surprised to find that you want to keep playing it yourself.

We've divided the book into sections for easy use: indoors, outdoors, on a journey and on the beach. However, many of the games can be adapted to work just as well in a different environment – a game for the car can work brilliantly in the park, or a beach game in your kitchen.

This book won't turn you into a 'perfect' parent, grandparent, step-parent, godparent or babysitter. But we hope it will give you the inspiration that you sometimes need to really enjoy your time with children. And there's nothing more important than that.

I'M BORED! ...

INDOORS

START WITH A SQUIGGLE

This is just the thing for those who feel like doing a bit of drawing but have no idea what to draw.

Get a piece of paper and a pen. Draw a squiggle, doodle, pattern or shape anywhere on the paper, making sure that a fair amount of room is left elsewhere on the page. Look at the squiggle, turning your page any which way you like, and see if you can turn it into the start of a new drawing. So for instance, draw some curvy lines as if you were drawing the top of a cloud. Then think of what else it could be: the top of a tree, a sheep, a friendly dinosaur with a bumpy back, a frog's head with bulgy eyes, etc. The top-half of a cloud turned on its side could be the beginnings of a monster's hand coming round a door. Held upside down, it could be the start of a comedy car with big bumpers and crooked wheels.

This game also works well if there is a group of children; everyone makes a squiggle and then hands it on to the person sitting next to them. If there is a baby or toddler around, then let them do all the squiggles – it makes them feel very important.

TENTS

There is no doubt that tents have a magical quality that gives most games or toys a new lease of life. Being able to close the curtains, play in secret and get up to all sorts of mischief without being disturbed will always spark the imagination.

First find a spare sheet or blanket or even an enormous dressing gown. Then get a couple of chairs and place them with backs facing a few feet apart, or find a table big enough to sit underneath. Throw the blanket over the top and crawl inside. To ensure complete privacy, make a sign to hang up outside that makes it very clear that this is a secret tent and that everyone else should keep out.

If the tent feels big enough, grab a couple of pillows or cushions to sit or lie on. They will immediately make any den feel very cosy, and if your children are recovering from a bug, or just feeling a bit small, it's the perfect place for a bit of quiet time with some books. Alternatively, if everyone is in a more lively mood, squeeze in as many toys or friends as will fit and hold a noisy tent-warming party serving pretend cups of tea or glasses of wine.

Tents make great museums too, housing the latest collection of jigsaws, cars or hairclips arranged in order of preference. The best thing of all though has to be finding that last bit of chocolate Easter egg that has been saved for ages and crawling into the cosy tent to eat it as quietly as possible, making sure that nobody hears the silver foil crinkling.

NEWSPAPER CUT-OUTS

This requires a little bit of preparation, but if your children like cutting things out, then this is the game for you.

Find an old newspaper or magazine or brochure and get everyone to cut out lots and lots of words. (It's often best to cut out a whole line of writing and then snip each word off individually.)

When you have amassed a really good pile of words, start to re-arrange the words to make a poem. It doesn't have to rhyme or scan, and can be about anything you want. (If you can't find a word that you really want to use, then feel free to cut out individual letters and put them close together.)

If you are feeling ambitious you could try a haiku — a Japanese poem which is exactly seventeen syllables long. Here's an example of a haiku: 'Play the fool and lift a heavy screwdriver to be prime minister.'

Another good use of cut-out words is to send an anonymous letter to someone. Traditionally used in movies as ransom notes, you could send something less threatening, like a note saying: 'Can you guess who loves you? Make me a fruit scone for my tea if you think you know who I am.'

For children who can't read, cut out photographs in newspapers and magazines. Stick them together, or draw on them, to resemble someone you know. Alternatively, you can cut out Tony Blair's eyes, Dolly the Sheep's nose, Jamie Oliver's mouth, Jennifer Aniston's hair and stick them all together to make a very odd-looking character!

If you have any leftover words or pictures at the end of this game, then put them in a box or envelope to use next time.

RAT-A-TAT-TAT

This is a great game for a group of children or it can be turned into a happy solitary pursuit. Just two things are needed. First, a container: something like a bucket, saucepan or biscuit tin. Next, some dried pasta, dried beans, marbles or little stones (which we call 'rat-tats') – anything small that will make a 'rat-a-tat-tat' noise when dropped into the container.

One of you is the 'rat-tat' dropper and everyone else must sit with their backs to them so that they can hear, but not see the rat-tats being dropped. Silently each of you must try to keep count of how many rat-tats have been dropped. Rat-tats can be dropped at irregular intervals so that some slow ones are easy to count and some fast ones are nearly impossible to guess correctly.

When the rat-tat dropper has finished, everyone says how many rat-tats they think are in the container. The rat-tats are then counted and the person who comes the closest is the next rat-tat dropper. Remember that you may hear some rat-tats bounce into the tin but you won't necessarily hear them bounce out of the tin.

If you ever hear rat-tats dropping in the same rhythm as 'rat-a-tat-tat' then you all have to shout out 'rat-a-tat-tat!' before continuing with the game.

To play on your own, stand an arm's length away from the container so that when you hold your arm straight out, your hand is directly above the bucket. Then begin to drop the rat-tats in one at a time and see how many you can get into the box in one go, without one bouncing out or missing altogether.

For a bit of variety, or if you need to handicap older players to even out abilities, try rat-tat dropping with eyes closed, whilst balancing on one leg, putting the bucket directly behind you rather than in front of you, using a smaller container, etc.

PICNICS

Make-believe picnics are great to play by themselves or as an addition to a camping holiday (see **Going on Holiday**). The only requirement for this game is a picnic rug. It doesn't matter how big it is, just find an old towel, tablecloth, tea towel or a snuggly blanket and lay it out flat on the floor.

Then think up all sorts of favourite things that people would like to eat on picnics – banana sandwiches, jam tarts, apples, crisps of course, tiny sausages, plastic cheese, ice creams with flakes in, roast chicken with bread sauce – whatever tickles the tastebuds.

Don't forget about real picnics indoors either. Picnics are fantastic if you want to do something a bit different at teatime when everyone is feeling bored and ratty. A tired-looking sandwich and a cut-up apple miraculously become the world's tastiest food if they are served up on a makeshift rug on the floor rather than at the table.

FEELY TIGHTS

This is a particularly good game for little ones.

Take a pair of thick tights that you can't see through, then get a handful of around-the-house objects (a mug, an apple, a toy car, a clothes peg, a fork, a pepper pot, a sock, a scrubbing brush, a lipstick) and stuff them into one leg of the tights. Then see if your child can tell what each object is just by looking, then feeling the outside, then putting their arm down the tights and feeling inside. If they still can't guess then you could give them a few clues.

A box of raisins or a biscuit packed at the very bottom of the tights is a good surprise.

TABLE FOOTBALL

This is a game for at least two players, and is probably not advised for anyone who is feeling a bit wheezy or suffering from a hacking cough.

Find a scrap of thinnish paper – a piece of old newspaper or magazine is just the ticket. Scrunch it up into a ball several times so that it begins to retain some sort of spherical shape. Next decide on your pitch – a clear flat surface is what you are looking for. Tables are ideal as it is obvious when the ball has gone out of play (off the sides and on to the floor) or when you have scored a goal (off either end and on to the floor).

Decide which players are on which team and make sure they know which goal they are aiming for. Everyone then puts their hands behind their back and one person is nominated to drop the paper ball into the middle of the pitch. Now the fun begins: everyone must blow the ball as hard as they can towards their goal and try to score. If the ball leaves the side of the pitch then it is dropped back into the middle of table roughly where it was before it left the table. If a goal is scored then it just gets dropped back in the middle. There is no point in being too precise in this game – it is determination and heavy breathing that wins here, not fairness and accurate passing.

If you have any straws in the house, you can try blowing through them for an interesting variation. They tend to give better control and direction of the ball.

TOP TIP: Do not play this game for too long – you can get quite dizzy.

GOING ON HOLIDAY

Everyone loves the thought of going on holiday, whatever age they are. It is very easy to get excited and imaginative with this game, which has no rules except that it has to be fun. Here are a couple of pointers to get you going.

First, decide where to go. Is it to be a beach holiday in Spain, a mountaineering adventure up the Himalayas, a pony-trekking jaunt in wet Wales, or a quick weekend away visiting an old aunt who lives in a haunted house?

Next, travellers will need to pack. This part of the game alone can often be extremely rewarding — favourite toys and clothes, however impractical, can be stuffed into a bag or suitcase. Holiday-makers should remember pants, socks, something to wear at a party, swimming goggles, riding boots or woolly hats and scarves (whatever is appropriate) plus bits of paper or books for passports and tickets. For extra authenticity, get someone to pretend not to be able to find the tickets and passports by slapping their pockets and saying 'I'm sure I put them right here!'

Now comes the actual travel part, so work out whether the journey is by plane, train, boat or bus. What can be seen out of the window? Are the seatbelts working? Is anyone allowed to go and help the pilot or driver for a bit?

Here are a few ideas of things to
do once you reach your imaginary destination:

• Change into holiday clothes.
• Jump off the bed into the warm sea and splash
  around, keeping an eye out for sharks or octopuses.
• Take the tired and faithful ponies around the house,
  stopping occasionally to let them munch some
  grass or drink water from a babbling brook.
• Get out a magnifying glass and spook-o-meter to
  see if there are any clues as to who is making the
  mysterious howling noises at nightfall.

Don't forget about the joys of a camping holiday
(see **Tents**). All food can be cooked on a pretend fire
just outside the tent, and opening up the buttons at
the bottom of a duvet makes an excellent sleeping
bag. Remember that everything seems to get damp

when camping, so be prepared to drape holiday clothes over bits of furniture to give them a good airing.

Drawing a postcard of an imaginary holiday is a great way to finish off the game...

STINKY MILLER

This is handy when you need a five-minute filler, for instance when everyone is seated and waiting for tea to appear or cool down.

Somebody starts by saying in a very serious voice, 'Someone here has made a stink, Let us all sniff the air and think.' Then they must sniff the air around them in a comical way (lots of piggy noises, lots of 'Pooooeeey', lots of rabbit nose-twitching), and then point at someone saying 'Was it you?' At this stage, the person who has been pointed at must shake their head, then they in turn say 'Was it you?' and point to a different person and then that person points to another person... and so on. Sounds easy, doesn't it? EXCEPT that all the time that you are pointing and asking 'Was it you?' absolutely nobody must smile or laugh. You have all got to look incredibly serious. If anybody cannot keep a straight face, then the game starts again with the person who laughed starting with the initial rhyme 'Someone here has made a stink...'

DEAR DIARY

Diaries, in our experience, are hard things to keep going. Father Christmas would bring us each one every year, and it would be diligently written up every night until about the end of February, before any early enthusiasm would wane and the diary turned into a notebook to play noughts and crosses in. Writing them became a bore, and our entries dwindled to what we had eaten for breakfast or that we were studying the Vikings in History (yet again).

However, there was one diary which was always fantastic, and that was a holiday diary. It was just an exercise book with flimsy paper but it would record the thoughts and feelings of the whole family. Anyone could write in it at any time. Mealtimes were good for diary-writing. We would pass it round and describe our best moment of the day, or something delicious that we had eaten, or why we had walked off in a huff and didn't want to join in that afternoon. We would also stick postcards in, and little sachets of sugar from a restaurant, or a ticket from an event that we had been to.

Reading these diaries again now gives us fantastic pleasure, not only remembering our own experiences, but those of our sister and parents and all of our cousins and grandmothers. And because we were all writing it, it was easy to keep going with it, taking inspiration from each other.

For younger children, it is a great project to get them to draw a picture in a diary with a few words to explain something that happened today: 'Uncle Rory came to tea... I saw a kitten... I ate a boiled egg... We went swimming.'

You don't have to be on holiday – you could do it just at weekends or over the Christmas break. Just make a note of what you were all doing, eating, thinking, feeling, playing, disliking, refusing to do...

HOMEMADE BAND

The more people there are to play this, the noisier and merrier it becomes, but you can easily play it by yourself and, what's more, you don't even have to be remotely musical.

Take a little look around the house and you will be amazed at how many musical instruments can be created. Here are a few examples:

- Put a handful of dried beans into a jar or an empty plastic bottle, replace the lid and shake to and fro in a groovy way. Instant homemade maracas!
- Take a wine glass with a stem. Put a bit of water in it and then run a wet finger around the rim, holding onto the base with your other hand. You may need to experiment with the speed and the pressure that you use in order to elicit a ringing note. You can line up lots of glasses next to each other, each with different amounts of water in them and see if you can play an actual tune.
- Find an empty bottle and place it just below your lips. Then blow in a gentle, slightly peculiar way, top lip a bit more sticky out than the bottom one. Different shaped bottles will make different notes, and you can also fill bottles with varying amounts of water to alter the sound.
- Saucepans turned upside down make extremely

good homemade drums to be banged with wooden spoons... particularly good for very young children. Pan lids make excellent cymbals.

- Stretch a thick elastic band over a door handle, pulling down with one hand and plucking it with the other. The more you stretch it, the higher the note.
- Fill a washing-up bowl with water and then take a metal saucepan lid and hold it by the handle so that it's vertical. To make a wobbly sound now start tapping the lid with a metal or wooden spoon while you dip the lid in and out of the water.
- Blow down the spout of a clean watering can. Blowing, in this case, means making a farty noise with your mouth. The watering can acts as a great amplifier.
- Take a rack from the oven, and then drag a metal egg whisk up and down it.
- Try sweeping a hairbrush over a sieve.
- If you have a comb lying around you can fold a piece of greaseproof paper over it, and then hum into it. This is a good way of keeping the tune going.
  - Gently slap your cheeks while you make an O-shape with your mouth. As you open your mouth wider the note changes pitch.

When you have set up your band and you are all ready to go, then decide on a song to play. Start out with something simple like 'Happy Birthday'. Swap around so that you each get a go on different instruments. You could put a CD on and play along with it too. When you have been playing for ten minutes or so, you will be good enough to enter the Eurovision Song Contest. Find some glittery eye-shadow and dance around energetically singing 'Eh Bia Bolla Bia Beh.'

KIM'S GAME

This is a favourite old party game that our great-granny remembered playing. We've also discovered how to play a version with really small children who can't write yet.

Take a large tray and place lots of household objects on it. Some should be straightforward like a mug, a cotton reel, a match, a leaf, a smartie, a toy car, a fork, etc., and some unusual like a rabbit's foot, a piece of ginger, a shoe that the dog has chewed, etc. Altogether there should be about fifteen items. Place the tray on the floor in the middle of the room so that everyone can see it, and leave it for one minute. If all the players are old enough to write, then give them pens and paper, and once you have covered the tray with a tea towel, ask them to list all the items that they can remember. Put a time limit on it (maybe three minutes); whoever has the most is the winner.

If you are playing with younger children, then show them the tray and get them to have a really good look. Then take the tray away, remove one object and show them the tray again. Whoever is first to guess which thing is missing gets a sultana. Repeat until tray is empty.

TOP TIP: When you remove the tea towel, do so with a flourish and a 'tan-naah!' They seem to think it's some kind of magic.

DRESSING-UP BOX

Although this is not strictly a game on its own, we thought it might be worth including a list of useful things to collect for a dressing-up box. Keep everything in a cardboard box, chest, bottom drawer or a bin liner in the attic.

Have a look through your clothes if you are having a bit of a clear-out. What you don't want any more could be a great costume for your children if you roll the sleeves up and put a safety pin in the back. Charity shops, jumble stalls and car-boot sales are also fantastic places to get cheap costumes. Here are some ideas of what to look out for:

- Old nighties (they make great princess outfits)
- Hats of any kind (pretty essential)
- Jewellery, beads, bracelets, chains, brooches, glasses, masks
- Anything with feathers, fake fur or tassels
- Large pieces of scrap material
- Old cushions for stuffing inside your costume to change your shape
- Bedspreads, blankets and sheets
- Sparkly, shiny clothes, fairy wings and wands
- Wet-weather gear
- Umbrellas, walking sticks, plastic swords
- Headscarves, woolly scarves

- Ribbons, belts, ties
- Old shoes and boots, clippy-cloppy shoes (essential)
- Old make-up

Once your children start dressing up, they will soon be off creating all kinds of fantastic characters and scenes, and it may be hard to convince them that they can't really go to bed dressed as a frogman with flippers on. Try and persuade them to put on a play instead!

SECRET CLUBS

This works best of all with two or more people, as secrets are really only fun if they can be shared. A secret club combines all that is good about being devious and exclusive with great invention. The thrill comes from knowing something that the grown-ups don't.

All secret clubs are different, but here are a few essentials:

- Firstly, they should decide on a name for their club. Get them to think of something that they like, or which makes them laugh, or are good at. For example: No Smelly People Allowed (N.S.P.A.), Dogs And Lollies For Ever (D.A.L.F.E.) and Cheese and Onion Crisp Haters (C.O.C.H.). Once they have settled on a name, and this may take a whole weekend, then it should be referred to by its initials only. And they should never tell anyone else what it stands for.
- Get them to think up rules for the club. For instance, always eat a sweet before lunch, no babies allowed, don't walk on the cracks in the pavement, only brush your teeth with your left hand. These rules should be enforced whenever the secret club is meeting.
- They might want to make up a secret password that

must be used if they want to come into the room, or a secret series of knocks if they call for each other.

- How about making up new names by mixing up the letters of their real names? For example, if their real name is Ella Beard, then their new name could be A Red Label. Or they can take their middle name followed by the name of the street they live in. Or they can write their name backwards and see how it sounds. (Yllop Ecila and Hannasus Esor!)
- Get them to make badges for all the members, bedroom door notices and posters. What about a secret handshake?
- If they're feeling ingenious then they could write to each other in a secret code. Codes can take a little time to set up, but once they all know what it is, they can send messages between themselves that no one else will ever guess.

It is worth pointing out that secret clubs can cause a bit of sulking from people who aren't allowed to join. If someone really, really wants to join an existing club, then suggest they can join if they can swear an oath of faithfulness and carry out a very difficult task, like going to the kitchen and sneaking a biscuit for everyone without anyone finding out. If they are still not allowed to join, then simply get them to start up their own secret club with someone else. Grown-ups love secret clubs!

NEWSFLASH

This is the silliest of games but it causes terrible giggles, especially if lots of grown-ups join in. Everybody writes down a sentence on a slip of paper and puts them into a bowl. These sentences can be anything you like, but in this game, the sillier the better.

Here are a few examples:

- 'The prime minister accidentally let out a really smelly fart when he met the queen today.'
- 'Joseph likes eating snails and worms.'
- 'Matilda took all her clothes off and ran around the supermarket wiggling her bottom.'
- 'Daddy won the world record for snoring and burping.'

If there are only a couple of you playing, then write four or five sentences each to keep the game going. Try not to be too rude, but in our houses, the words fart, poo, bottom, and wee-wee are all acceptable, and very hard to say in a serious voice.

Then one by one each person must take a slip of paper from the bowl, put on a very grave face and pretend to read the news. You start by saying, very slowly, clearly and solemnly, 'Good evening. Here is a very important newsflash,' and then read the sentence out loud. The difficult bit is that you must not laugh. In fact you must not even titter or smile. Everybody else can laugh as much as they like, but the newsreader must keep a straight face. Then you pass the bowl to the next person for their go.

This game can be played just for the fun of it, but if you want to have a winner then you could have a rule that if you laugh three times during the game you are out.

HIDE AND SEEK

It seems absurd to forget this favourite game, but for some reason we still manage to overlook it at times, and we are sure we are not the only ones. Please don't ignore it – it is a cracker that works well for all ages of children.

If you need a reminder of the rules, one person (or however many people want to) counts up to a chosen number within their grasp of numeracy. Everyone else goes off to hide, either together or in different places. The counter then shouts something like 'Ready or not, here I come!', and goes off to look for the others.

Good places to hide: behind curtains, under duvets and pillows, behind sofas, under beds, in cupboards, on a messy hallway floor covered in coats, behind doors (but watch out for fingers), under the kitchen table, lying down very flat in an empty bath, anywhere in the garden, or in a big dirty washing basket (if you can bear the pong).

Bad places to hide: anywhere that you have to squeeze yourself into so tightly that you will not be able to squeeze your way out again, or anywhere that involves trying to move a heavy piece of furniture.

If the seeker is having a hard time finding anyone, he may request the hiders to call 'cuckoo' or give a little cough to help him in his search.

TOP TIP: Always go to the loo before you start to play this game. What is it about hiding in small spaces and having to be quiet that makes you want to have a wee so badly?

DOCTORS AND NURSES

Yes, yes, yes, we all know this one. In our experience, this is usually a race to see who can get completely undressed the quickest and then lie around on the floor getting cold. But it doesn't have to be like this. If you or your children fancy an alternative version, here are some ideas to start you off.

Firstly, you all have to decide who is going to be the doctor and who is going to be the patient. If there are a few of you playing and a squabble is developing over whose turn it is to be the doctor, then don't forget how important nurses are (and they get to wear great uniforms). There can also be numerous student doctors who can watch the doctor first and then copy (particularly good for younger children who are unsure exactly what to do).

Patients are equally important and can make loud sicky, coughing, painful noises while they wait their turn to be examined. Soft toys and dollies make silent but excellent patients too. We used to spend hours lining up all our dollies making endless lists of disgusting-sounding ailments as we examined them, covering them in red felt-tip pen dots which were supposed to be rat bites. (The felt-tip never properly washed off though, so don't let anyone make that mistake.)

To get imaginations going, it can help if you gather

together a few bits and pieces first. Raid your bathroom cupboard for some cotton wool, maybe a spare plaster, an orange stick or nail file, a medicine spoon, a compact mirror, anything that vaguely brings to mind a medical kit. You only need one or two blunt implements to check belly buttons, armpits, nostrils or whatever seems to be the chosen medical specialist area of the day. Don't forget a roll of loo paper if you can spare one – it makes brilliant bandages, which are surprisingly strong.

Make sure that you all know a good long list of things to check – the obvious such as heartbeat, pulse, temperature, ear, nose and throat, broken bones and any particular sore part of the body – but also think of some rarer complaints such as crocodile bites, missing fingers that need sticking back on, a lumpy tummy, a cut on the back that is oozing purple goo, etc.

Some smaller doctors and nurses may need prompting with their beside manner. Doctors always ask what they can do for you today, how long has it been hurting, does it hurt when I press this, make an appointment to see me in a week's time. Nurses are very good at holding hands, providing comfort, asking more general soothing questions such as, 'Have you got any brothers and sisters?', 'What is school like?', 'Have you got any worries about the operation?', and they are always excellent at giving injections and medicine.

DOUGH MAKING

Most people have in their kitchen cupboards the answer to a cold, grey, rainy day. Playdough and saltdough are made by mixing the cheapest of ingredients, and you will save yourself a fortune and have a lot of fun if you make your own.

To make playdough, put the following into a pan:
    200 ml/1 cup water
    125 g/1 cup plain flour
    150 g/$^{1}/_{2}$ cup salt
    2 tablespoons of cream of tartar
    2 tablespoons of cooking oil
    A few drops of food colouring
    A drop of vanilla essence (this is not essential, it just makes it smell better)

Heat gently over a low heat, stirring until it makes a dough. It takes less than a minute, and you can store it in a plastic bag in the fridge for months.

Playdough is fantastic for younger children to squeeze and mould. Let them roll it out, cut shapes, poke with forks, and discover how it squishes between their fingers.

If you have older children bored of just making sausage shapes, give each of them a piece of paper with an animal or object written on it, give them a two-minute time limit, and see if they can guess what each other has made.

To make saltdough which can be baked in the oven, mix together the following ingredients in a bowl:
200 ml/1 cup water
275 g/1 cup salt
275 g/2$\frac{1}{2}$ cups plain flour
1 tablespoon of cooking oil

Knead the dough onto a floured table, and model into shapes. You may need to add a little more flour if it is very sticky.

Once the dough has been successfully moulded, bake on a tray at 180°C/350°F/gas mark 4 for about twenty minutes. After cooling on a wire rack, the cooked dough can be painted and varnished.

Favourite things to make are: food for a dolls' house; animals; figures to inhabit Tracy Island, Christmas crib, farm, fortress, railway station; cave for Action Man to hide in; baskets for Beany-Babies to sleep in; initials or even the letters of your whole name to go on a bedroom door.

TOP TIP: Aunties just love birthday presents made from saltdough – so much better than another boring bar of lemon soap.

HAIRDRESSERS

OK, this game has one rule that everyone must always stick to: NOBODY IS EVER ALLOWED TO REALLY CUT ANYONE'S HAIR.

Right, dire warning over, playing hairdressers is really good fun.

The best way to avoid any trouble is to pretend that your fingers are scissors, but cutting hair is not the only thing hairdressers do. There is washing and blow-drying, and putting in curlers. And don't forget brushing, although do be gentle if your customer's hair is a bit on the knotty side.

If you have some hairclips, scrunchies, twisties or hairbands, then styling is the most inventive thing that you can do with hair. Try trying it up on the top of the head, with a few loose bits hanging down; or what about two bunches, or lots and lots of plaits? Dads can look great with a bit of a brush and a carefully placed pink hairclip.

Hairdressers love to chat, so be sure to ask lots of questions. For instance:

- 'Been anywhere nice on your holidays?'
- 'How's that boyfriend of yours?'
- 'Did you see Coronation Street last night?'
- 'You still living in that big flat with all the Australians?'

If there are two or more of you being hairdressers then you can ask each other things like:

- 'Michelle, have you seen the wide-toothed comb?'
- 'Do you mind if I leave a bit early today to finish my Christmas shopping?'
- 'Julie, could you get that phone? I'm up to my elbows in dandruff shampoo.'

THOOP!

This is a firm favourite with two-year-olds, but it does need a bit of supervision to prevent too much tasting. And be prepared for a bit of cleaning up afterwards. Place your two-year-old in the middle of the kitchen floor with a pan to make the thoop in. Then give him or her anything in your cupboards that you can spare. Some dried pasta, dried beans and lentils, a cup of flour, old bits of celery, a pepper grinder, sugar, breadcrumbs, apple cores, banana skins, rice. A little bit of anything will suffice. Then make sure that he or she is wearing clothes that are expendable, give them some water, and some cups and spoons and whisks... and stand back. There! Now you can make that telephone call you've been trying to make all morning.

MAGAZINES

If you want a project to last all day, all weekend or even all holiday, then this is the game. It's fun to do alone or in a group, and the possibilities and variations are endless. Making magazines could be the start of a lucrative career, or it could just be something to smile at in a few years' time. Either way, make sure the finished magazines are kept in a safe place to treasure later on in life. Pens, paper etc. are needed, and it's good to staple the magazine together at the end.

Here are some suggestions for budding journalists:

- Talk to someone for an **interviews page**, asking them what they would like to do if they won a million pounds. Don't forget to ask tricky questions too. Or pretend to interview someone famous... and make up the answers! Find a photo of the celebrity in a newspaper and stick that on the page as well.
- Draw some pictures of clothes for a **fashion page**, and write a bit about why the outfits are so cool.
- Make up some letters for a **problem page** and then answer them in an unhelpful and patronising way. Things about love, spots and what happened at breaktime are usually really juicy.
- Review the top 10 hits at the moment for a **music page**, and write about whether they are any good or

not. (If anyone is caught saying 'How can anybody listen to this mindless rubbish?' or 'Whatever happened to lyrics?' then they have become a grown-up without realising it.)

• Include a photo or postcard of somewhere that you have all visited for a **travel page** and write a bit about the journey, whether the hotel was any good, etc.

• Create a **sports page**, listing how many cups and medals a favourite team has won. Profile their best players: how they got where they are today, their strike rate, their wives, how much money they earn and their haircuts.

• Include a recipe for something simple like a sandwich or peppermint creams for a **food page**. Write a review of today's lunch, rating the meal with stars, and comparing it with food at other people's houses. Or try out three different fruit drinks, describing which one is best and why.

• Give a run-down on the state of the family pets for a **pets' corner**, describing what the pets have eaten, how many poos they have done, how smelly their cages are etc.

• Pretend to know what lies in store for people today and make up some **horoscopes**. Things like, 'It's a good day to make important decisions', or 'If you are horrible to your brother today a dragon will come and eat you up.'

- Stick in a few photos or hand-drawn pictures of friends and family, then make up a bit of juicy gossip about who they were seen with last night, drinking champagne until dawn and then falling out of a taxi!
- Write down any useful bits of information for the **top tips page** (often the funniest), like how to curve a football into the back of the net, or what colours look nice together, or how best to annoy a sister, or how to kill ants by pouring hot water onto them.
- Make a **cover**. This will have a drawing taking up most of the page and some headlines letting the reader know what will be inside. It is best to leave writing these to the end when the contents have been decided. Keep them short and make sure they grab the reader's attention!

CUPS AND KNICK-KNACKS

This is basically a memory game that can be adapted very easily to suit the tastes and abilities of all those playing. In essence, pairs of things (we call them knick-knacks) are hidden under whatever cups or bowls are to hand. Small knick-knacks are best, so go for two coins, two corks, two lumps of sugar or cheese, two bits of apple, two pieces of pasta, two Smarties, etc. (In fact, this game works well just using Smarties alone and pairing up the matching colours — it's a good way of making a packet last for ages.)

Start off with about ten assorted cups and bowls and, turning them upside down, shove a knick-knack under each one. Then swirl them around like a magician and start the game. Each player is allowed to lift up two cups to see if the knick-knacks match. If they don't match, then replace the cups and move on to the next player. If they do match then you get to keep (and maybe eat, if you're lucky) the knick-knacks, and have another go. Keep playing till all the knick-knacks have been matched up, but don't remove the empty cups or the game is too easy...

FAMILY DISCO

It's six o'clock, you've all had tea, it's not quite bathtime, and the kids need more bouncing before bed. This is an all-round excellent thing to do to break up any tension in the house. You only have to dance for about five minutes and everyone will be laughing and exhausted. So here we go.

Put on some music. Good, boppy disco, or some funky soul, or something jolly and folky. Actually, it doesn't really matter what you play, as long as it makes you want to jig about a bit. If it is appropriate, let the kids work the CD player (all those brilliant buttons!), then... dance! We mean really dance. The more you jump around and swing your arms, the more everyone will love it. And remember, this is a family disco, so unless they have a very good excuse, the whole family must join in. If you have small children, sit them on your shoulders as you dance (watch out for door frames!) or hold their hands and let them stand on your feet.

Then, when you're all getting warm, the tallest person shouts 'Hey, man!' and does a special dance that everyone else must copy. This might be hopping on one leg, clapping hands in the air, slapping their bottom, doing monkey arms, or all of these at the same time. Then, when everyone has got the hang of this particular dance, the tall leader shouts 'Groovy!'

does a spin and points at someone else, who in turn shouts 'Hey man!' and becomes the next leader making up a new move for everyone else to copy. You get the picture? Hey, man... Groovy!

Make sure that at all times you give each other plenty of encouragement: 'Nice move'... 'Funky footsteps'... 'Dig that shimmy'...

HANDS DOWN

Good for three or more people.

Find one small coin or small object. One of you is the chooser and must shut their eyes while everybody else silently decides who is going to hold the coin. The chooser then opens their eyes to be presented with a mass of clenched fists to choose from. Look carefully at everyone's fists and scrutinise their faces for signs of guilt, deception or embarrassment. If you have any suspicions about a certain fist you can ask its owner to do something with it. For instance you can say, 'Suzy, please scratch your nose with your left hand,' or 'Granny, please pretend to shake the maracas with your right hand.' Players must carry out whatever order is imposed on them as long as they can do it with a clenched fist. If you are not holding the coin and are asked to do a task, feel free to try and make it look as if you are the one holding the coin, to confuse the chooser.

If, after five commands, the chooser is still none the wiser, then they have one last chance. Find a flat, hard surface such as a table. The chooser then shouts 'Haaaaaaannnnds down,' and on the word 'down' everyone must slam their palms down flat on to the surface. If you do it quickly enough, the coin should stay hidden and may not make too much of a clang as it hits the surface. If you do it too slowly, the coin may poke out from beneath your hand. The chooser must then decide which hand hides the coin. No winners, no losers, just start the game again with a different chooser.

THE HAT GAME

This is best played with a group of you, but it can be tailored to suit any age. As each round of the game lasts exactly one minute, you may need to find an egg timer or a watch with a second hand on it in order to ensure that nobody gets longer than their allotted time.

Firstly, set yourselves up with some paper and pens. Tear some paper into smallish pieces and hand out ten or so pieces to each player. Everyone then writes down one word on each bit of paper. They can be simple words like cat, ball, green, jump... or they can be more difficult like washing, magic, woolly, lampshade. Occasionally you can put in a real stinker like perpendicular or kazoo. Then fold up the papers and put them all in a hat.

Next, organise yourselves into pairs or teams and decide who is going to go first. That person then gets the hat, pulls out a word and describes it to their team in any way they like. They can use words, noises, actions, anything at all, as long as they don't say the word that is on the paper! The object of the game is to describe as many words as you can in one minute, before you pass the hat on to the next team. Don't put guessed words back in the hat, but if your minute is up and you have an unguessed word in your hand don't tell anyone what it was, fold it up and put it back.

For instance, if the word is lampshade, then you can say 'Oh blimey, that's difficult, um... It's the thing that goes... um... over the top of, the... er... thing that you switch on, at night, when it's um... dark, and it's sometimes made of paper or something... Oh blimey... Look! That thing there!' as you finally point at a blasted lampshade that was there all along. But you mustn't say lamp or shade.

Meanwhile your team are shouting out any answers as they think of them, as well as helpful comments like 'Oh come on for goodness sake! Does it have any legs? Is it alive? Hurry UP will you, time's running out!'

It's easy to play this with children who can't read or write yet too. Someone can whisper the words to them before they have a go at describing them, and some older players may have to write a few extra words on their behalf at the beginning of the game.

TOP TIP: If you put too many really difficult words in, you are just as likely to have to describe them as your opponent is. You have been warned!

PUPPET SHOWS

Our children have some stuffed toys and dolls that they hardly ever play with. If this rings a bell in your household then a puppet show is a splendid way to get those neglected toys down from the shelf. We used to love doing this as children. Perhaps it's something to do with imagining all your teddies are alive, or just an early tendency to do silly voices and show off a bit.

The sofa is the place, a rainy afternoon is the time. The puppeteers hide behind the back of the sofa with the aforementioned teddies, dolls, Action Men and of course puppets, if there are any. Then they choose a story. It's quite good to start with a story that everyone already knows, like 'Cinderella', or 'The Three Bears'. They should then decide which of the toys is which character and, keeping well hidden below the back of the sofa, hold up the toys, doing different voices for them, acting out the story.

It might be worth suggesting that they practise the story once or twice before asking someone to come and watch.

Audience members should be encouraged to cheer and hiss, order large gin and tonics for the interval, and to heap loads of praise on the exhausted performers at the end by saying, 'Darling, you were simply maaaarvellous!'

MATCHBOX SQUEEZE

A really simple game, which seems to enthral younger children in particular.

Find a matchbox, empty out all the matches and then go round the room collecting as many different tiny things as will fit into the matchbox. The person who fits the most things in is the winner; or, if there is only one person playing, get them to try and beat their personal best.

Ideas for things to squeeze into a matchbox: coins, a cornflake or rice crispy, a marble, a bit of fluff, a Barbie shoe, a hairclip, a bead, a button, a piece of pasta, a grain of rice, a tiny drawing on a tiny piece of paper, a blade of grass, a leaf, a stone, a sultana, a cotton-wool ball, a spider, and a match of course!

DICKENS AND JONES

This game is all about being very grown-up and pretending to work in an office as a secretary. We used to spend hours pretending to be Mrs Dickens and Mrs Jones, the faithful, efficient and rather bossy secretaries to our imaginary boss, Mr Hamilton. It's perfect for slightly older children who love their new set of felt-tip pens and want to do something other than a drawing.

A couple of key items are needed for this game. Firstly, a table to sit at and something that each person can use as a telephone. Mrs Dickens and Mrs Jones had the most incredible red phones that lit up whenever they rang, but any toy phone or even a loo roll with some numbers drawn on it will do. A pen and paper is also essential for writing down lots of phone messages, ticking boxes, making lists and underlining <u>very important words</u>!

Next, work out what sort of office it is. Junk mail can be an excellent source of inspiration. Here are a few examples of what we mean.

- A magazine from an estate agent... Give imaginary callers advice about properties, and arrange viewings. Remember that estate agents are famously untrustworthy and frequently tell fibs.
- Takeaway pizza leaflets... How much is a

Hawaiian? Do you want extra olives with that? Sorry, we don't deliver more than three streets away.

- A Barbie catalogue... The pink shoes are £7.99. Delivery will take ninety days. Oh no, sorry, we've sold out of that item.
- We had an old school prospectus, so we very often pretended to work in a school office taking tricky calls from teachers and parents.

Whenever anyone wants their phone to ring, they just need to say 'Bbrring, Bbrring' and then think of an appropriate way to answer the phone, e.g. 'Hello, Mrs Dickens here, how can I help you?' or 'School office, Mrs Jones speaking. How can I help you?' or just 'Mr Hamilton's office.'

When the phones aren't too busy it's a good time to talk about sandwiches, films and holiday plans. Don't forget to fill out those stationery order forms, and be careful not to smudge any imaginary nail varnish as you flick through telephone directories and count huge piles of paper ten-pound notes...

SMELLS FAMILIAR

This game is fantastic fun, but as always, a little supervision is probably safest.

There is generally a good collection of things to smell lying around the house. Go round the house looking carefully in each room. How about some perfume, a teabag, a bar of soap, an orange, suntan lotion, a nasty old cleaning cloth or a rotten old trainer? You want to aim for about ten things that have got a definite pong about them, some good pongs and some bad. DO NOT COLLECT GLUE OR CLEANING PRODUCTS.

Now either trust someone to keep their eyes tightly shut or blindfold them. When you are sure they can't see, carefully lift each smelly item to their nose and ask them to take a big sniff. You score a point for every pong they can't guess, and they score a point for each pong they can.

If you are feeling really brave, you can move on to level two of this game: Tastes Familiar. This time you will be collecting things for tasting, so for safety confine your search to edible things only. Try tiny amounts of vinegar, salt, sugar, lemon, toothpaste, ketchup and coffee as well as banana, cheese, honey and other scrumptious things.

TOP TIP: Always have something delicious as a reward after tasting something disgusting.

BATHTIME

Water is a source of great excitement for most children. But if, like us, you feel that bathtime is sometimes incredibly hard work, and that you have run out of energy, ideas and occasionally the will to live, here are a few pointers to help you get through the final furlong.

- Blow bubbles.
- See how many small plastic animals will fit on one plastic boat, and play Noah's Ark until it sinks.
- With two or more children, have a soup race. See who can finish a small bowl or cup of water first, using only a spoon to drink from.
- Line up a few choice plastic Teletubbies or Action Men and squirt them until they are knocked over.
- See who can make the tallest tower on the edge of the bath with rolled-up flannels, plastic bottles,

sponges, toys, boats, soap dishes and whatever else you have floating in the bath.

• Trickle cold water down the backs of anyone not brushing their teeth properly.

TOP TIP: Endless cups of bathwater tea, with bathwater milk and bathwater sugar go down much better if you have a real glass of cold, white wine at the same time.

POTATO PEOPLE

A particularly good pastime for younger children, this is also good for using up old green potatoes and soft, manky apples that no one fancies.

First, assemble an assortment of fruit and veg that are not going to be eaten. Then find some matchsticks. Cocktail sticks are good too, but are a bit spiky so BE CAREFUL!

Now make people out of them. If you can find a small potato with sprouts coming out of it, then that would be an excellent head with either a sprouting nose or sprouting hair. Secure it to a body, which might be a bigger potato, or an apple or even an orange, using a matchstick as your link. If you have any old carrots, they make good legs and arms. If not, then use matches again, to make little, weedy, thin limbs.

It's best to make potato people sit down, as they balance more easily. A good felt-tip pen will draw in eyes. How about a sultana that can be secured with half a matchstick to make a nose or mouth or some tangerine-peel hair? Do your potato men look like anyone you know?

TOP TIP: If you leave your potato people on a plate on the window sill, quite soon they will start to wrinkle and go mouldy, making them look even better. But they get a bit smelly after a week, so don't forget to throw them away and not leave them behind the curtains all summer, like our cousin Ben who found maggots all over his potato dinosaur!

BUFFY AND GRAVY

A good game for lots of you. Everyone playing sits on a cushion, gets into a rough circle, and thinks up a dog's name for themselves, except for one person who stands in the middle, whom we shall call the dogwalker. Our dogs were called Buffy and Gravy, hence the name of the game; you can, of course, call your dogs anything you wish.

Go round the circle and shout your dog's name out to the dogwalker. Then woof, pant and get down on all fours. The dogwalker then chooses two of the dogs' names, gets down on all fours as well and calls out the two chosen names as if they were calling their dogs from far away, e.g. with a bit of whistling beforehand or in a very strict voice.

If your dog's name is chosen, you have to crawl as quickly as possible, wagging your pretend tail, and try to swap places with the other dog before the dogwalker gets to one of your vacant cushions in the circle. Whoever doesn't make it to a space gets to be the next dogwalker.

If at any time the dogwalker shouts 'Walkies!' then all the dogs have to crawl around and find a new place. The last person to a new space gets to be the dogwalker.

For extra laughs and confusion, try playing it with a couple of real dogs – they love it.

SLAPPERS

You can play this if you have an old newspaper and some empty floor space. It's an excellent game for using up a spare bit of energy, and very good for getting rid of irritation and annoyance. Each person takes a large sheet of newspaper and rolls it up, not too tightly, into a baton shape. Then someone who is responsible enough to use a pair of scissors takes another sheet of newspaper and cuts out fish shapes for everyone, about ten centimetres long. You can colour in your fish if you want to, so that you know which is which. Now place your fish at a starting line, decide where the finish is, and slap the ground behind your fish to (hopefully!) move it forwards. Lots of slapping is needed, and your fish won't always go in the direction that you wish, but keep going, and someone will eventually make it to the end!

Try different shapes; starfish are good and very unpredictable. Or draw around your foot and cut that out.

Draw sheep shapes and try to herd them through an open door together, calling 'Cum Bye',

'Gin Jen' and whistling through your teeth, à la 'One Man and His Dog'.

CLUEBY-DOOBY-DOO

There are treasure hunts in other sections of this book which are about trying to find lots of things from a long list. These are great if you are outdoors, or on a beach. But when you are indoors, and have access to paper and a pen you can play another kind of treasure hunt, which we have called Clueby-Dooby-Doo.

First, think up what the treasure can be. A handful of gold chocolate pennies is great, or a wrapped-up birthday present. You will know best what your own children would like to find. Hide the treasure well – it is amazing how sharp those young eyes are when they really want to find something.

Then you have to work backwards. On a small piece of paper, write a clue that will lead to the treasure. For instance, if the treasure is hidden under the dog's bed, the clue might read, 'A flea-bitten friend who likes biscuits will rest his weary head here.' Then, hide this dog-bed clue somewhere else, maybe in the flour jar. Then write a clue that will lead to the flour jar, like 'If you want to bake a cake you'll have to sieve me first.' Then hide this flour-jar clue somewhere else, maybe tucked into the back of the telly. Then write a clue that will lead to the back of the telly... You get the idea? Keep going for about ten clues, and make them as cryptic or as simple as you wish, depending on the age of the children playing. If the weather is good, don't forget to hide clues out in the garden too. Hand over the last clue that you wrote to start your hunters off on their quest.

This game does take a bit of preparation, but it really is worth it. And once your offspring have learnt how to lay the trail, they can do one for you. The clues that they write are usually much harder!

CONSEQUENCES

There are lots of variations to this classic game. Here are our favourites.

Each player needs a sheet of paper and a pen or pencil that actually works. In our house this is sometimes the hardest part of the game.

The simplest version of Consequences goes like this. Each person draws the head of an animal at the top of their page. It can be a real animal, or a made-up monster with, for instance, three eyes and loads of spots. Then they draw a neck, fold down the top of the paper so that only the neck is showing, and pass it on to their neighbour.

Next, everyone draws a body, connected to the neck. It could have arms or wings or tentacles or spikes – it's up to you. Leave an indication of where the legs begin, and then fold down the drawing and pass it on again. Finally, draw legs and feet of any kind. When everyone has finished, pass it on again, open up the drawings and look at the extraordinary results.

Story Consequences is a bit different. This time, instead of drawing, you write down a boy's name. It works best if it is someone famous, or someone in the room, or someone that you all know. Then fold down the name and pass it on. Next write 'met' followed by a girl's name, again someone you have all heard of. Fold down and pass it on. Next, write 'at' followed by a place (funfair, swings, cinema etc.). Fold and pass. Then 'he said' (fold and pass), 'she said' (fold and pass), and finally 'and the consequence was' – this can be anything you like: 'They were married and lived happily ever after' or 'She hit him on the head with a wet fish and never spoke to him again!' Open them all up and read them out to each other.

RAIN ORCHESTRA

A game for a truly wet day, not light indeterminate drizzle. Also probably a game for bored younger children, but older children are always very good at helping and bossing the younger ones around. Choose a spot just outside your door where big spots of rain are splashing on the ground. Very often a porch roof or leaky gutter provides a perfect steady stream of ploppy rain.

Then get some containers – pots and pans are great, plastic bowls, potties but probably not the best china, and line them up either the right way up or upside down where the rain is good and splashy.

Then all you have to do is listen, listen, listen from inside the house and you will soon hear the different noises that your very own rain orchestra is making. You might even feel like singing along.

I'M BORED! ...
OUTDOORS

PICK-A-STICK

Any number of you can play this, or you can do it on your own, slowly and methodically. Collect up sticks of all different sizes and lengths – maybe twenty sticks in all, more if there are lots of you. Make sure they are all vertical, then let them fall to the ground so that they fan out and make a pile at the same time. Now take it in turns to remove a stick from the pile without any other sticks moving. If you are successful, then have another go. If any other stick does move, even a little bit it is the next person's go.

If you want to make it more difficult, you could use only your left hand if you are right-handed, or vice versa. It's also harder with gloves on. The winner is the one with the most sticks at the end, and the prize is to choose which tree to climb.

FAIRY HOUSES

These work best of all in some woods where there are plenty of sticks, leaves, moss and old trees with deep roots.

Your fairy house can be as elaborate and sophisticated and imaginative as you like. Make one in a team, or go off on your own so you'll have the freedom to do exactly as you want with it.

The key to a successful fairy house is to find the right sticks. What you need are two sturdy sticks of roughly the same length, which are forked at one end, and three more good solid sticks of a reasonable length. Choose a sheltered nook at the base of a tree in between two roots where you think the fairies might like to live. Then position your fork-shaped sticks as upright as possible with the two prongs parallel to the tree trunk. Put two more of your sturdy sticks in between the trunk and the prongs of your front forks to make the edges of the roof. It helps if you can somehow wedge these side supports into little craggy holes in the bark. Place your last sturdy stick across the front of your roof. Now all you need is a handful of twigs and sticks to form a messy criss-cross pattern on the roof. Then collect the final layer of roofing, which can be moss, bracken, grasses or leaves, and cover the roof carefully to provide an idyllic shelter.

Now comes the really fun bit, furnishing the house. Think about pieces of bark or flat stones for a table, something the fairies might like to sleep on (fairies aren't fussy if their mattresses are hard or soft), a bit of moss or leaves for bed-covers, maybe some food and plates to eat off. Acorn cups make very good wine glasses, and snail shells are excellent fruit bowls. Can you find something to become a tiny bath or a kitchen sink? Make whatever seems right for your fairy house. Don't forget a chimney. We always used to dig a little hole nearby for the fairies to use as a loo. You can also build a garden and a path in front of the house. What about a swimming pool and trees? If you have tiny children wanting to join in, it's not a bad idea to set them to work on the garden, as the houses themselves can be accidentally knocked down by less agile hands!

PEBBLE FOOTBALL ALL THE WAY HOME

This is a cracker for getting tired people to walk that tiny bit further to get you all back home, or to the car park, or wherever you are aiming for.

Any willing players should pick a stone or pebble, not so small that it is impossible to find again, and not so big that it is only going to travel a few inches every time you kick it. You want to be able to kick the stone while you are walking, without breaking your pace, and for the stone to go ahead of you by ten to twenty feet. Keep your eyes fixed on it so that you simply forget how much walking you are doing in between each kick.

It obviously helps if you are playing this game on a track or path that is gently sloping downhill, but you can still play it to help you get up a hill, although you will have to kick your pebble football many more times as it will naturally keep rolling back towards you.

LADYBIRD GARDENS

These are really good fun to make, but quite fiddly. Be prepared to get earthy fingers, and to give up a few flowers from the garden. If you are making a ladybird garden in the fields and meadows, be careful not to pick too many precious wild flowers. Ladybird gardens are harder to make in the park, but you could give it a go if there are lots of daisies. It works best if you are in the garden, where you are allowed to pick a few petals or flowers, and have access to a couple of things from indoors.

You can start off in two ways. Either find a flattish container – a seed tray is perfect if you have one, otherwise, any container with low sides, like a serving dish, or a shallow-sided cardboard box, will do. Or, if you are nowhere near a container to make it all in, you could clear a little area of the ground, and put some sticks to mark out the boundary fence, or stones to make a wall.

Fill your container with earth from the garden, or sand from the sandpit, and pat it down smoothly. Then use some small stones to make a winding path, some little leaves and flowers to make bushes and plants. See if you can make a tree out of a twig with some leaves on, or use a bit of moss to look like foliage. One of the best features in our ladybird garden was a pond, made from a pot or lid sunk into the soil, lined with tinfoil and then filled with a little water. We used to float a petal on it to look like a water lily. Can you make some garden furniture? Try using a peice of bark as a bench or table, and some snail shells as chairs. Do the ladybirds need a little vegetable garden? With a spade and a fork? If you are feeling very clever you could work out how to make a swing or a hammock. Or make a nice finish to it by making a gate or a little arch as an entrance.

TOP TIPS: 1) Make sure everyone knows which flowers and leaves are OK to pick, as some are poisonous, and some are stingers.
2) Watch out that cats don't mistake the beautiful ladybird garden for a litter tray and use it as a loo!

WALKIE TALKIE

Walks. Why can it be almost impossible to get a capable, energetic six-year-old to go that final hundred yards to the car park? Or seemingly  able-bodied eleven-year-olds willingly to join in a family ramble through the woods? Our children sometimes used to feel that walks were a chore to be endured, occasionally rewarded at the end with a packet of crisps and a fizzy drink in a pub car park. Until we all invented Walkie Talkie.

This is a magical way to keep everyone's interest going for as long as you need to, and used to make us squeal with laughter. Grandparents are especially good at this, as you can never be quite sure if they are telling the truth.

All you have to do is ask questions. You can ask anyone anything. It's really up to you whether you tell the whole truth, or whether you make up a fantastical response. The key to the game is to be informative and imaginative. There are no material prizes in this game, but you do get a lovely feeling while you are munching your pork scratchings at the pub if you think that you've found out something new and useful.

Here are some questions for children to ask adults:

- Did you like school? What were you good at? Who was the naughtiest person in the class?
- What actually is your job? What do you do all day? If you didn't have to work what would you do?
- What is the most dangerous thing you've ever done?
- What makes you scared?
- What is the naughtiest thing you've ever done?
- Have you ever lived in another country? Would you like to live there again?
- What was Mummy/Daddy like when they were my age? Which of my aunts and uncles was the naughtiest? Did you fight with your brother?
- Who is your best friend?
- What was it like when you got married? Did you ever get married before that?
- Have you ever been to hospital? Have you ever had stitches?
- Why do you get cross if I don't tidy my room? Did you tidy your room when you were little? Honestly?

And here are some for grown-ups to ask children:

- Who is your best friend and why? Have you ever had an argument with them?
- Would you rather live in the town or the country? What do you like about it?
- What kind of pet would you have if you could have anything at all? What would you call it?

- What's your favourite thing about school? And your least favourite?
- What makes you scared? Angry? Laugh?
- What's the most exciting holiday you've been on?
- Did you by any chance spot where I put the car keys?

SEVENS

You will need a ball for this game, and a wall or garage door to bounce it against. A football, a tennis ball or a beach ball are all fine. A cricket ball is not so good as it's too hard and doesn't bounce very well. You can play on your own, or take it in turns with any number of players.

SEVEN times, throw the ball against the wall and catch it.

SIX times, throw the ball against the wall, let it bounce on the ground once and then catch it.

FIVE times, bounce the ball on the floor with the palm of one hand (like a basketball player) and then catch it.

FOUR times, bounce the ball off the floor, then off the wall and then catch it (the opposite of Sixes).

THREE times, throw the ball against the wall, clap

your hands twice and then catch it.

TWO times, throw the ball under your leg, bounce it off the wall and then catch it.

ONE time, throw the ball against the wall, turn right around and then catch it.

There are plenty of ways to vary Sevens – touch the ground, do it with one hand, stand on one leg, stand further away from the wall each time. We used to play 'Stillses', which is where you have to keep your feet in exactly the same spot, except for lifting up one leg for Twoses, and turning around for Oneses. See what variations you can come up with.

STUCK IN THE MUD

Be prepared to get dirty hands and knees in this game. The more people you can get to join in, the better. Decide on boundaries for the game, so that no one wanders off and gets lost.

One person is 'it' and they must chase the others and try to touch them. If you are touched (even a tiny little touch!), then you must stand up straight with your arms above your head and your legs apart. You can be freed only by another person crawling underneath your legs and out the other side. The person who is freeing you is 'safe' and cannot be caught while actually crawling through.

We sometimes play a version that is called Melting Candles: when you are caught you stand in the same way, but you slowly sink to the ground, making it harder to be freed. If you end up collapsed and melted on the floor, then you become an 'it' as well, and now try to catch the others.

When everybody is stuck in the mud with no one left to free them, a new person can be 'it'. Or you'll be exhausted and stop anyway.

If there are lots of wheezy adults playing, then we suggest that you mark out a little patch with sticks or sweaters (or it could be a park bench) and call it 'home'. This is a safe place where you cannot be caught. However, only one person at a time is allowed in there. If someone else jumps in then you must jump out, even if you have only been there for two seconds. Sometimes it just isn't fair, but then that's the game!

BILLY GOAT SPLASH

This is a game of daring and bleating. Choose someone to be the troll, and the rest are goats.

Place sticks on the ground to form two parallel rows, about six feet long and two feet apart. If you can't find sticks, then use a couple of sweaters, coats or rows of stones instead. This is the bridge. At one end of the bridge place a pile of treasure – about fifteen different things which need to be collected. This could be shoes, or pennies, or conkers, or apples, or pebbles, or coloured leaves... whatever you have to hand. Probably not boulders.

The goats sit at the other end of the bridge to the treasure, bleating 'baa... baaa!' The troll sits close to the side of the bridge with his eyes closed and his back turned, so he cannot see the treasure, the goats or the bridge. Then one of the goats must try to creep over the bridge to collect a piece of treasure and get back to the herd without being heard. The other goats must carry on bleating to try to disguise any trit-trot sound of hooves.

Meanwhile, the troll must listen very carefully. When he thinks that he can hear a goat on the bridge he shouts 'SPLASH!' and turns around to see if he has caught anyone. If any part of a goat is on the bridge then they are kidnapped, and must go and sit by the troll. However, if there are no goats on the bridge then the troll must give up a piece of treasure.

The game ends when all the treasure has been collected or all the goats are captured.

The goats can try to trick the troll into thinking that there is someone on the bridge by bleating extra loudly, or making running noises with their feet. And if the troll succeeds in catching all the goats he may of course sing 'I'm a troll, fol-de-rol' and proceed to eat the goats for his supper.

BUG RUMMAGING

In most woods, gardens or along country lanes, you can rummage for bugs by turning over a stone, flowerpot or pieces of bark and logs. In one single bug-hunting expedition recently we found centipedes, earwigs, spiders, ants' nests, an orange slug, millipedes, beetles, worms and woodlice galore. Anything that you don't know the name of is called an ibboo.

Have a pokey stick handy, and if, like Suzy, you are not too fond of creepy crawlies, then try to be brave. Soon you will discover that they're really not so much frightening as fascinating.

MAKING A DEN

As children we made some dens that were so ridiculously dangerous it's amazing we're here to tell the tale. There was a particularly precarious log house, supremely engineered by our cousin Sophie, with big, heavy planks on the top. Kelvin Wheatcroft kicked it down while we were inside it. We escaped with a few bruises, but unfortunately Kelvin was the victim of a mysterious attack later that summer at a village disco. Some angry girls put a blanket over his head, stole his trousers, and threw them into the pond. Poor Kelvin had to run all the way home in his pants, while the girls hid behind the bus shelter laughing!

Building a den is the very essence of childhood. A secret place, where adults are only permitted by invitation. It can be stuffed full with 'borrowed' items, like Granny's best quilt and a few cushions, a plastic yoghurt pot filled with stolen raspberries, and crisps and sweets of course. We even made fires and boiled eggs from the hen house for our tea. It was the very pinnacle of independence for nine-year-olds.

How you make a den depends entirely on the materials available. If you are in a small back garden, you can sling a blanket or sheet over the washing line and secure it on either side with stones or logs. If you are out in the park, you might find a branch hanging down low that you can turn into a hiding place with some coats. An umbrella makes an excellent roof. But if you have the great good fortune to be in the woods or fields then there will be a wealth of natural building materials: fallen branches, logs, sticks, leaves, bracken, grasses, stones, hay bales and much more. If you can purloin some bin liners to put on the ground, you won't get such a wet bottom when you sit down.

Please tell your children never to light fires without someone responsible with them, but do let them cook a sausage supper, or toast marshmallows on long sticks. It's a memory that will last for ever.

WHAT'S THE TIME, MR WOLF?

This is a huge success, particularly with little children, whose squealing and excited giggling must surely be one of the best sounds in the world.

Choose one person to be Mr Wolf, while the rest of you are sheep. Make a line on the floor and get all the sheep to stand behind it. Mr Wolf stands with his back to the sheep, about ten yards away.

All the sheep then call out 'WHAT'S THE TIME, MR WOLF?', and whatever o'clock he calls, the sheep must take that many steps towards him. So if he answers 'Seven o'clock!' they must each take seven steps, 'One o'clock!' means one step, and so on.

When the wolf judges that the sheep are pretty close behind him, and he is asked the time, he can shout out 'DINNERTIME!' He then whirls round and tries to catch the fleeing sheep, who must run back to the start without being caught. Any sheep that is captured becomes a wolf too. Continue until the last sheep is caught.

TOP TIP: Really young children like to hold someone's hand so that they don't get too frightened, and can be helped back over the line.

BOAT BUILDING

If you are lucky enough to be having a day out by a babbling brook, then here is a gorgeous way to while away an hour.

Make a little boat. The very best ones that we've ever made were fashioned out of good pieces of bark, but you can also try small bits of branch. With some types of soft wood you can poke a stick in to make a mast. A large leaf threaded onto a twig makes a fine sail. You can then race your vessels down the stream. Poking with long sticks is allowed if your boat gets stuck on a bank, or tangled up with some weeds, but pushing your boat downstream is cheating!

At a recent Barratt family party, cousin Dylan gallantly waded waist-deep to keep everyone's boats in the main channel, while the rest of us kept beautifully dry feet running through the meadow following the race.

We're sure you don't need to be reminded, but ALWAYS supervise children playing in or near water.

TODDLER'S DELIGHT

If you are going on a walk with a very young child – one who can walk pretty well but who has a tendency to want shoulder rides – here are a few tips on how to have a successful jaunt. Most of these diversions work with older children too.

Go slowly. Look ahead all the time for something to take their interest, and then get really interested in it yourself.

A few examples include:

- Thistledown to blow off their hand, like fairies
- Blackberries to pick and eat
- Snails to find under flowerpots
- Four-leafed clover to search for

- Trees to climb
- Beetles and slugs to inspect
- Dandelion clocks to blow
- Stiles to negotiate
- Huge leaves to use as fans
- Sticks to throw really far
- Low walls to walk along
- Steps to jump up and down
- Branches to bounce on
- Gates to open and close and climb over
- Puddles to jump in
- Horses to pat
- Cows to moo at
- Sheep to sing to

If you have a dog lead or a bit of string, tie it onto yourself and let them pull you along. Or tie it loosely round their middle and pull them up a hill. Let them win a race to the next corner. Sing 'The Grand Old Duke of York'.

The key is to be in the same frame of mind as them. It doesn't matter if it all takes a bit longer. If you let them know that you are in a hurry, they will almost certainly drag their heels more!

It's different, of course, if you have older children with you too, but if you have the luxury of an hour outside with a toddler, then go at their pace, give in to their ideas and rediscover the joys of carefree, idle busyness.

HUGGING TREES

This is the point at which accusations of old-hippiedom are likely to start flying, but hugging trees is a really pleasurable experience. Teenagers particularly should be encouraged to do this, as it has a curiously calming effect. Our mum was often muttering wishes up to the branches as she clung to a tree trunk with her eyes closed, and she definitely felt better for it. Give it a go. It'll make you smile.

Find a tree that you like the look of. Big oaks and beech trees are especially fine, but a small silver birch sapling has its own allure too. The texture of the bark will change from tree to tree, and so will the temperature, depending on whether the sun is shining on it or not. Now wrap your arms around, press your cheek against it, and have a little think and a wish. Look up at the branches above, and the leaves blowing in the breeze, and the puffy white clouds scudding across the sky. Breathe deeply and feel the benefit!

POOH STICKS

Made famous by A. A. Milne and the Winnie the Pooh books, this enduringly popular pastime is still a winner.

Location is pretty essential here. You need to be standing on a footbridge with a river or stream flowing beneath it. Size doesn't matter. We've played it on big lock bridges over the Thames and a tiny stream in North Wales with a stone slab over it.

Each choose a stick. Compare them so that you can distinguish between them from a distance, e.g. 'Mine's the long one with a twiggy bit at the end.' Stand on the upstream side of the bridge, then, after a count of three, all drop them into the water. (You're not allowed to cheat and aim them under the bridge like our cousin Pippa always did!) Then run to the other side of the bridge and see which stick comes out first. There seems to be no advantage to having a big or small stick, or which bank you stand closest to. Keep going with new sticks until everyone has won at least once. You can also use leaves and bark. Try not to fall in, and hold the hands of small children very tightly.

SKIPPITY SKIP

We used to get such bad giggles playing this. A pretty silly game, but one that we still enjoy.

One of you gets up and skips from A to B and back again to A, while saying out loud, 'Skippity skip, skippity skip.' Everyone else must watch, noting carefully every single move and noise you make. Notice how the person skipping holds their arms or how long it takes them to turn around. Maybe they nearly lose their balance at one point or have to stop and cough. Clock their facial expression – what are their eyes and mouth doing? There is only one rule: when you are skipping, you must concentrate and do your finest skipping.

The skipper then sits back down again and nominates someone else to copy them. The chosen person must do their very best imitation of the last skipper, trying to remember everything that they did, and exaggerating, of course. It is then the imitator's turn to skip properly and another's chance to mimic.

HARES AND HOUNDS

This event needs lots of you and a little bit of preparation. But it is fantastically good fun, and leaves everyone exhausted and ready for a huge lunch. The Barratt clan is exceptionally good at this game.

A large number of people is what is needed; anything over four will work, but if gets really exciting when there are nine or ten of you. Two people who know the area are chosen as the hares. Then they set off, running if they can, but certainly going at a brisk pace. They take with them a bag of flour, or hay, or sawdust, or finely shredded newspaper, which will decompose over time, and lay a trail as they go, putting a little pile of whatever they have about every thirty yards. If they want they can leave arrows made from sticks on the ground.

After about fifteen minutes everyone else can set off. They are the hounds, so if the hounds at the front of the pack find a pile of flour they bark, howl or bay to let the stragglers know which direction to follow, and also to let the hares know how close they are getting. If the hares want to, they can lay a few false trails, doubling back on themselves and going off in a new direction. It's also worth putting a few Crunchie bars in an obvious place (e.g. on top of a stile, at the foot of a tree or next to a pile of sawdust). The chocolate serves both as an incentive for the hounds, and as a tactic to slow them down while they share them out. Sometimes the hounds will catch up with the hares; sometimes the hares will make it to the pub, or back to the car, or home, first. If you only give them a five-minute head start it's pretty even. The point is not winning or losing, but eating chocolate, running till you are really out of breath, and having extra roast potatoes and gravy at the end of it all.

BONKERS FOR CONKERS

OK, so you have all had fun collecting conkers. But what do you do with the shining brown beauties stuffed into every pocket?

Instead of skewering the conkers (and yourself) on bits of string to make vicious knuckle-rappers, keep them in your pockets for the rest of the afternoon and carry on your walk until you find a suitable place to rest a while. Then look around to see if there is a puddle, a thick branch or the trunk of a tree, a small patch of mud, anything that you can use for target practice, and toss your conkers at your target, scoring out loud as you go. You can either all fire at the same target or have individual ones, but make sure no one is too near the target – conkers really hurt if they get you in the wrong place.

Polly's son, Jojo (being a typical boy and mad about anything that he is allowed to throw), once spent an entire afternoon trying to throw conkers into a bucket after he had got home from the park. When he ran out of conkers in his pocket he simply went up to the bucket, tipped it upside down, refilled his pockets, uprighted the bucket and started all over again, and again, and again...

GRANDMOTHER'S FOOTSTEPS

This is such a classic and a winner for younger children.

One of you is Granny (preferably Granny if she is around, or maybe a grown-up for the first game while everyone gets used to it). Granny stands twenty feet or so away from all the others with her back turned. While she is not looking, everyone must silently creep towards her. Whenever she turns round, all of you must stop moving immediately. If Granny sees any feet moving at all, she can order their owners back to the initial starting point and they will have to try creeping up all over again. There are no rules as to how many times she can turn round, but she should allow enough time in between turns for everyone to take a couple of steps. Whoever manages to reach Granny first and tickle her, gets to be Granny in the next round. Remember: it is only feet that must not be seen moving — the odd sway or correction of balance is allowed.

We played an excellent version of this game after a

magical picnic in the middle of some bluebell woods in Dorset. All the grown-ups were feeling a little sleepy and so were allowed to lie down on the rugs with their eyes shut. All the children gathered at a tree about thirty feet away and had to creep up on us, without us being able to hear them. If we heard any whispering or any twigs breaking under their feet, they all had to start again. They loved it and we got a few minutes' kip in the sunshine – perfect.

52 BUNKEROO

This game conjures up so many happy memories. We were incredibly fortunate to grow up having access to a huge communal garden. We spent every summer evening in huge gangs, chasing each other through long grass and stealing secret kisses from our childhood sweethearts. Even the inevitable hay fever and awkward heartbreak couldn't quench our thirst for this game – plenty of running, plenty of shouting, and plenty of opportunities to hide secretly with other people.

First of all, choose your 'base'. This needs to be an obvious place that you can run to – a big old tree, a park bench, a pile of jumpers on the floor, anything you can call base. One of you is 'It', stays at base with their eyes shut and counts fairly swiftly to fifty-two.

Everyone else has to run away and hide. Choose your hiding place well. You want to be able to peek out now and again and see what It is up to and where they are in relation to the chosen base.

When It has finished counting, they must have a good look and wander around a bit to see if they can see anyone hiding. If they do spot someone, they must run back to base and shout '52 Bunkeroo, I see Ella over by the long grass.' Ella must then walk back to base and wait. If, however, Ella has already realised that she has been spotted, she can try and race It back to base. If she touches base first, she can shout '52 Bunkeroo, I'm in' and is safe. At any stage of the game, anyone who is hiding can hedge their bets and try to run for base if they think they can get back before It spots them running and makes for base as well.

Inevitably, people do get caught in this game – it's easier being It than being one of those who hides. The first person to be caught is usually It in the next round of the game. However, there is a chance that you can be rescued. Here's how. Once all of you bar one are back at base, you can shout 'SAVE ALL' to the last hider. They will then know it is crucial that they get back to base, proudly shouting '52 Bunkeroo, I save all,' before It does, thereby rescuing everyone. It's easy to see why gangly adolescents suddenly turned into heroes on those long, hot summer evenings.

LET'S GET DIZZY

This is real belly-laughing stuff. Nearly all kids love being made dizzy either by aeroplane acrobatics or roundabout action. But here are a few more ways to make yourself and your kids dizzy which might be kinder to your back and their shoulder sockets.

Put your finger on the end of your nose and direct your eyes to it so that you are practically cross-eyed. Keep your eye on the end of your nose and ask someone to help turn you around five times (adult brains may need ten spins to reach maximum dizziness). As soon as you have completed your five turns, take your finger off your nose and run to a designated person ten feet or so away. Make sure you are on soft ground – one of you is bound to fall over in collapsed hysterics.

If you can't quite get the end-of-the-nose idea, then simply put your arms out to the side and bend over so that your chin is practically in line with your knees. Keep looking at your feet as someone helps to propel you round as quickly as possible.

Other good things to try after five or ten turns: jumping, hopping (impossible), balancing on one leg, a somersault or just lying on the ground staring up at the sky (hey, man).

HUNT THE SHOE

This will absorb smaller children when you are in a fairly overgrown area or on a nice patch of grass surrounded by bushes. If you haven't got enough energy or inspiration for a full-blown treasure hunt then take the fabulously lazy option. Kick off your shoes, pick one of them up and find a crafty place to hide it – in the long grass, up a tree, sticking out of a bush, wherever.

Make sure everyone who wishes to join the hunt has their eyes closed and backs turned so that they will not be able to see where the shoe is hidden. Then sit and observe while everyone goes off to search for the shoe, giving clues and signs of encouragement if needed.

FOLLOW MY LEADER

An excellent way to get children to walk up that hill or go just that little bit further. Try this before you resort to piggybacks or chocolate bribes.

Form a line, one standing behind the other. The first person in the line is the leader and starts walking. After about five paces, the next person starts walking, then the next after another five paces and so on. If the leader decides to start marching, or striding slowly, or walking with their hands out to the side, then the next person in line should do the same, followed by the next person, etc.

Other good things to try as the leader include:

- Hopping
- Wiggling your bum around
- Clapping
- Singing a TV theme tune or advert
- Jumping
- Smelling a particular flower
- Walking as if your legs are giving up
- Blowing raspberries
- Leaping over a stile

It doesn't matter what you decide to do as the leader, but try to fit in something different to do every twenty paces or so.

When one person has had a good enough go at being the leader, send them to the back of the line and start again with a new leader.

DAISY CHAINS

A good quiet pastime that needs just three things – daisies (obviously), patience (sometimes hard to come by) and a good-length fingernail. We suspect that girls like making these more than boys do.

Pick two daisies, each with as long a stem as possible. Make a cut with your fingernail about halfway up one of the stems so that it looks a bit like an eye of a needle, i.e. there is still some stem surrounding the cut on all sides. Then thread the other daisy through the cut, being very careful that you do not rip the stem. Then make a cut in the stem of the daisy you have just threaded through and find another long-stemmed daisy to go through that cut. Keep going and make a bracelet, necklace, tiara or garland.

Very often it's not the daisy chains themselves that are the pleasure of this game. It's the conversations you have with your children while you are all busy with your hands, nobody necessarily looking at each other, just peacefully sitting down and helping each other out. Younger kids are fantastic at finding the daisies and concentrating on long stems, while older kids with more agile fingers love creating the finished line of jewellery.

GARDEN OBSTACLE COURSE

Obstacle courses are best done individually, with each racer competing in turn against the clock, seeing who can achieve the best time. Set these courses in the park or woods, and especially in the garden. Here are a few things that you could put into your course:

- Crawl under a garden chair
- Run backwards carrying a bucket of water
- Do a somersault, cartwheel or walk on your hands
- Jump over a watering can
- Walk along a wall, or balance on some upturned flowerpots
- Run around a tree
- Jump up or down steps
- Run in a pair of wellies much too big for you
- Crawl through a pile of leaves
- Put on a hat, scarf and gloves
- Do a three-point turn on a tricycle

Make certain that the course is properly set up each time, and be sure to have a go yourself. Your kids will like to see you falling over and looking silly!

WHACKY RACES

When you have had enough of normal running races, tried hopping, jumping and racing backwards, have a go at some of these.

Crab race: Get into pairs and face your partner. Both bend down, bottoms upwards, and grab hold of each other's ankles. Then race the other couples to a finishing line going sideways, without letting go. So while one of you is moving to the left, the other is going right.

Push-me-pull-you race: Stand back-to-back with a partner and link arms, then race other pairs up to a point and back again. On the way back, whichever one of you was going forwards now has to go backwards, and vice versa.

Spider race: Choose a partner. Crouch on all fours, then have your partner crouch on all fours over the top of you, but going across your back with their body, so that it looks a little like you have eight limbs. Then scuttle together around a circular course trying to gently knock into other spiders and distract and divert them.

Wheelbarrow race: Get into pairs. One person puts their hands on the ground, and the other one stands behind and picks up their legs. Together you race to the finishing line, trying not to fall over and bump your nose in the mud.

Pebble knees: This is a race in which you place a pebble about the size of a satsuma between your knees and then run. If your pebble falls to the ground you must start again.

Tortoise race: One person must be the judge and stand aside whilst everyone else is blindfolded and gets down on all fours at the starting line. When the judge says so, all tortoises should start to crawl as slowly as possible towards the finishing line. However, you must keep moving at all times. The judge is allowed to tell you at any time that you are remaining too motionless and, if deemed necessary, ban you from the course and turn you into a charming, but rather useless, antique cigarette box.

The aim of the race is to be neither the first nor the last to cross the finishing line (hence the need for blindfolds, so you can't see where everyone else is in relation to you). Thankfully, this means that you can have plenty of winners.

After the race, the tortoises can decide whether the judge was good and fair or too bossy, and are officially allowed to push the judge onto the ground and tickle until he or she apologises.

TREASURE HUNTS

We've included treasure hunts in other sections of this book because they are such fantastic things to do. The basic rule is that each person or team is given a variety of things to find. You can write lists and hand them out if you wish, or just call out a new object to look for each time something is found.

Here are some examples of things to choose from if you are out and about, in the park, garden, woods, fields or mountains:

A red leaf, an acorn, a fir cone, a fruit, a feather, a curved stick, a stick with a forked end, a wood louse, a rabbit dropping, a bit of wool, a bit of eggshell (no stealing from nests!), some moss, something blue, something beginning with M, a dandelion clock, a flying insect, a piece of straw, something that will hold water, something that someone has dropped, four blades of grass that are equal lengths, a daisy, a buttercup, an icicle, a singing member of the Von Trapp family...

HIGH JUMP

A little cheating is needed when playing this with young children, but those with long legs and good co-ordination should be able to manage it.

Find a stick about six feet long. Two people must then hold it a few inches off the ground, balancing it lightly on their fingers so that if it is knocked it will fall off. Each jumper then takes a run-up and tries to leap over the stick without knocking it off. Raise the stick a little higher each time, and see who can jump the highest. The cheating part is that, as very small children approach and take off, the stick-holders lower it almost to the ground and lift it back again once the child is over. Make sure the stick-holders get a chance to jump too, if they want to; some people, like Suzy, hate high jump.

When you have had enough of high jump, do a limbo dance instead. Start with the stick high, and go under it belly-up. Lower the stick each time, and see who can get under the lowest. You are supposed to go under with your chest facing upwards all the time, but the under-sixes that we know don't seem to be able to get the hang of it, so let them do it however they want!

UNDER-EIGHTEEN-MONTHS TODDLE OR CRAWLING RACE

This is exactly what it sounds like. We've included it because we wanted to remind everyone that really small people respond to races as well as larger ones, and that there are plenty of ways to ensure that they stand a good chance of winning. Either everyone has to copy the toddler's style of walking or everyone has to crawl, depending on which stage of development the youngster has reached. Crawling backwards often feels surprisingly strange and difficult, particularly with a hangover. Anyone who feels like a more experienced walker can always try to remember how to walk on his or her hands instead.

BIRDS' NESTS

If you can find the right kind of bendy sticks, young children adore making birds' nests.

Weave, bend and mould sticks into a small circle, and take it from there, adding grasses, moss, twigs, horse hair, wool and leaves. At Easter we like to make a nest to hide chocolate eggs in.

GRANDPA'S SIXPENCE

You can play this game if you are a grandpa, granny, aunt, uncle, godparent or just looking after a friend's kids for them. It does need a moment of preparation, but the delight on a small child's face is worth the effort.

If you have the grandchildren coming to stay with you, decide in advance where you might take them for a little walk. This could be to the shops, or woods, or park, or just down the garden. Then, some time beforehand, hide a small coin in a secret place: maybe under a stone, or brick, or in a tree trunk. As you approach it with your young brood, weave a story about how fairies live near here and sometimes leave money under this special stone. Elaborate as you see fit. Then let them look in the hiding place and find the treasure.

If you are fortunate to have the same children staying regularly, they will soon make visiting the fairy stone an essential part of their exciting stay. Even if they have an inkling that fairies don't really exist, they will love joining in with the possibility that maybe, just maybe...

I'M BORED! ...

ON A JOURNEY

THE IMITATION GAME

Perfect if you are waiting on a station platform or in a busy airport lounge where there are loads of people to watch.

One of you is the spy. The spy secretly decides whom they are going to imitate, choosing somebody nearby that they can watch. Then they surreptitiously copy every movement of the person they have chosen. Maybe they are reading a book or newspaper. Maybe they are eating a sandwich or pacing up and down. Maybe they are carrying a bag in a particular way or using their hands while they are talking or continually picking their nose.

The others have to watch the spy and try to guess who it is they are imitating.

If you want, you can also play this en masse, with all of you being spies at the same time and taking extra care that the person you are copying doesn't notice you.

ONE AT A TIME PLEASE!

This causes great mirth, and is particularly good when going at a fast pace. It doesn't matter if you can't sing in tune.

Choose a song that everyone knows, and go round the car, or up and down the queue, or across the train compartment, singing just one word each. For instance, the first person sings, 'Twinkle', the next, person sings 'twinkle', the third person sings 'little', the next one sings 'star', and so on.

A harder version is to sing just one note each: so, the first person sings 'Twin', the second sings 'kle', the next sings 'twin' and the fourth sings 'kle', etc.

Christmas carols are extremely successful, as are nursery rhymes. Celine Dion songs do not work well.

You can also try to tell a story using the same method. Each person says only one word, trying to make some sort of sense as they go. The smaller members of your family may well surprise you with their extraordinary off-beam thoughts, sending the story into previously undreamt-of avenues.

WHO ARE YOU AND WHAT DO YOU DO?

This is a tremendous game for traffic jams and queues, i.e. it helps if you are relatively stationary with nothing better to do than gape at people.

Choose any person you can see, and then try to imagine the following things:

- What is their name?
- What do they do for a job?
- What is their favourite subject at school?
- Where do they live?
- Where are they travelling to now?
- Have they got any children, brothers or sisters?
- Do they look happy, and if not, why not?
- Have they been arguing?
- Have they been waiting a long time?
- Have they ever been told off by a policeman?
- What is their dream?

Try not to let them catch you staring at them, and try not to be too cruel.

MIAOW! SQUEAK! HUOOO!

A noisy version of an old favourite, the 'Stone, Paper, Scissors' game.

You can play in pairs or threes, and score a point each time you win.

After the count of three, you all have to make a noise and a gesture. You have three options:

- You can squeak like a mouse and make your teeth go goofy.
- You can miaow like a cat and show your claws.
- You can trumpet like an elephant and pretend your arm is a trunk.

In this game, cat beats mouse, elephant beats cat, and of course, mouse beats elephant. If two of you do the same animal, it's a draw.

First person to ten points is the winner. The prize is one Hula-Hoop.

I WANT A RHYME IN DOUBLE-QUICK TIME

Smaller children, who love rhyming simply because they like the sound of words, will enjoy this game.

One person begins by saying 'I want a rhyme in double-quick time, and the word to rhyme is...' and then they choose whichever word first comes into their heads.

Say the word is 'JELLY'. Everyone else thinks of something that rhymes with jelly and shouts it back as quickly as possible. (You can go round in an orderly fashion making sure that everyone has a turn, but quite frankly it's not as much fun as shouting out spontaneously.) So, 'WELLY', 'SMELLY', 'TELLY', 'BELLY', 'UMBRELLY', 'GEORGE MELLY', 'THE LOCAL DELI', whatever you fancy, all get called out.

The person who chose 'JELLY' in the first place then gets to decide which rhyme they like the best, and whoever yelled it out is the winner for that round. The winner then picks the next word for rhyming and the game starts again.

NUMBER PLATES

Brilliant in slow-moving traffic jams, this game is a mixture of observation, invention and alphabets for all ages.

Take a look at the other vehicles around you. You will notice that most number plates will have a group of three letters, say BTM or VNS. Each person in the car must call out a word that begins with the first letter and has the other two following at some point. For instance, BTM might be bottom, bathroom, or bitumen (if you have someone really clever in the car...). VNS might be vans, violins or visitations.

There's another version of this game, which is to make up a relevant phrase using the three letters as the first letters of your words. For instance, BTM might be Big Tired Mummy, or Bus Trip is Magic. It's OK to add little words (at, in, the, to, of, a, and) to make it sound right. Younger children find this version easier.

If you are stuck in stationary traffic and have run out of new number plates to look at, then reverse the letters and see what you come up with. Or you can just make up groups of three random letters. Try taking the letters of your name and making up a suitable phrase to describe something that is happening. FREDDIE becomes Fly Round England and Don't Dither In an Emergency!

CELEBRITY SPOTTING

These days it seems that you can hardly avoid celebrity superstars behaving badly and feeling a bit emotional in airport lounges, so keep your eyes peeled, and you never know, you might just see a member of a boy band wearing his hat all wonky, looking constipated and doing that funny pointy thing with his thumb and forefinger.

But if you aren't lucky enough to see any real celebrities, why not play this game? You don't have to be in an airport lounge. It's good at train stations and on ferries too.

It's all a question of looking out for look-alikes. For instance, if you see a thin woman with dark hair, sunglasses and a couple of children, she's obviously Victoria Beckham. If you see a rather round person in a purple shell-suit carrying a handbag, it's probably Tinky-Winky. An old person wearing a wig? Elton John of course! And, wait a minute, who's that woman with big teeth and sensible clothes? Could it be... why yes! It's Princess Anne. Actually, we were playing this once and it really was Princess Anne.

IF I WERE KING...

This game is wonderfully inventive, but everyone needs a sense of humour and a willingness to join in to make it work.

Choose who is going to be king or queen first. Then complete the following sentences however you like. Always start with the words 'If I were King/Queen...' and then add:

- ... I would eat ...
- ... I would be able to ...
- ... I would wear ...
- ... I would have the power to ...
- ... I would go to ...
- ... I would make you ...
- ... I would make a rule that ...

Just imagine, you can eat chocolate all day, wear your spangly shoes even when it's raining, go to Timbuktu and ride on a jet ski. Or read the Sunday papers undisturbed. Meanwhile, each time you complete a sentence, everyone else around you must smile ingratiatingly and say nice things to you. It might go a bit like this.

King says, 'If I were King I would have the power to... jump over tall buildings so that I could get to my friend's house really quickly.' Everyone else says, 'Oh yes, Your Majesty. What a good idea, Your Majesty!'

Or, 'If I were Queen I would make a rule that everyone in Year Four is allowed to take their pets to school every day.' 'Splendid idea, Your Majesty, how brilliantly clever you are!'

They even have to say nice things if you say something like, 'If I were King I would make you all lick my shoes clean and do all my homework and feed me Twiglets all evening.' 'Of course, Your Majesty! Ooh, it'd be my pleasure, Your Majesty! Excellent choice, Your Majesty.'

Make sure everyone gets a go at being King or Queen, and the more bowing and scraping everyone can manage, the more light-hearted it will be.

GIRL, BOY, ANIMAL, PLACE

A good choice for twelve-year-olds who have a bit of knowledge and a competitive streak, but are beginning to drift into teenaged surliness and ennui. It works with the whole family too, although little kids might need a bit of help.

Pick a letter. One way to do this is for someone to say the alphabet to him or herself, at any speed they like, until someone shouts stop. Then they reveal which letter they had reached.

Let's say it was L. Starting with the next person, everyone takes it in turns to call out a girl's name beginning with L. Then a boy's name, then an animal (including birds, fish, mammals, insects, amphibians, and mythical creatures if you like), then a place (village, town, city, country, continent, river, mountain, forest, beach). All beginning with L.

If you came up with X, it might be better to choose another letter. If you get stumped you lose one of your three lives. No repeating. No squabbling. Take it in turns to go first, and to choose the letter.

BLIND MAN'S BLUFF

This game works very well in a car, coach or train, but is slightly trickier on a boat or plane, where the scenery doesn't change so quickly.

Choose someone to be the bluffer, and then everyone else must close his or her eyes. And NO peeping! (For obvious reasons the driver must NOT close their eyes, but they can be a superb bluffer.)

What the bluffer must do is describe what is going on outside the car, and see if they can slip in a few fibs without the others noticing. For instance, they might begin: 'Well, outside at the moment it's sunny with a few clouds and we're driving down a winding road with beautiful trees on either side, there's a magpie on the left-hand side of the road, and a phone box just coming up on the right and in front of us now is a hay lorry so I'll need to slow down a bit, and climbing on top of the hay is a lion who is pouncing onto the bonnet of the car...'

Obviously by now someone will have shouted out 'BLUFFER!' and will score a point for noticing the lie. Ten points earns a sweet. Continue until you have run out of fibs and Fruit Pastilles.

HOW MUCH IS THAT DOGGY?

When you have had enough of Old Macdonald and his increasingly repetitive farm, try a few verses of this.

How much is that doggy in the window?
WOOF WOOF!
The one with the waggly tail,
WOOF WOOF!
How much is that doggy in the window?
WOOF WOOF!
I do hope that doggy is for sale,
WOOF WOOF!

Two-year-olds are particularly good at the woofs.
Then change the animal that is for sale, the word waggly to something appropriate, and the noises will have to change too. Here are a few examples:

- A sheep has a woolly tail and says BAA BAA!
- A horse has a swishy tail and says NEEEEIIIIGH!
- A cow has a black and white tail and says MOO MOO!
- A pig has a curly tail and says OINK OINK!
- A camel has a pooey tail and spits.

We're sure you'll come up with lots more.

CRINKLY CRISP PACKET

A pastime for those aged somewhere between three and six months old.

Place unopened crinkly packet of crisps in the hands of baby. Then drive all the way from Northumberland to Devon while the baby finds it squealingly, endearingly funny.

YES AND NO

In this game you mustn't say yes and you mustn't say no.

Someone asks questions, like 'Are you hungry today?' or 'Do you want to lie on a beach and go swimming?' And the person who is answering must think of clever ways of giving an appropriate response without actually saying yes or no. You can't just nod or shake your head either. Try answering, 'That is correct,' or 'I am,' or 'It is.'

TOP TIP: This works well if an adult does the asking, and the more quickfire the questions are, the better. If a four-year-old is the questioner it can take rather a long time until anyone is caught out.

CARRY-ON KARAOKE

A top-favourite game, this one. Great hilarity. It is best played in the car with a radio or tape-player, although we have also found that on some long-haul flights you get headsets and piped music.

Turn on the radio or tape-player. Choose a tune that you know. It might be a nursery rhyme or Robbie Williams or a bit of Wagner's Ring Cycle. It doesn't matter if you don't quite know all the words, as long as you can remember the tune, and keep singing something!

Turn it up so everyone can hear and sing along. Then, when everyone has got into their stride, turn the sound right down until it is silent. Meanwhile everyone continues to sing, trying to keep exactly in time with the silent radio. After about twenty seconds or so, quickly turn up the volume and see how close you are.

This can be played with everyone singing at the same time, or with individual rounds. Little ones might like to sing in pairs.

DING DONG SPLAT!

All the family can play this. It's good if an adult starts the story-telling, but once they've got the hang of it, kids love being the narrator.

Tell a story. It doesn't matter what it is about, it can be a fairy tale that everyone recognises, a true story, or just something you make up as you go along. Spooky stories that aren't really scary are always a hit in our car.

As you tell the story, include lots of noisy things that happen, and everyone else must do the sound effects.

Good, rowdy things to include in your story include: doorbells, dogs barking, footsteps, eating spaghetti, creaky doors and floorboards, laughing, sneezing, coughing, corks popping, bottles pouring, rain falling, thunder, trains, owls hooting, waves breaking, muffled voices, police sirens, camels letting off, glass breaking, cows mooing, trumpets playing, helicopters, motorbikes, horses trotting by and many, many more.

You can either have each person take a turn in doing a sound effect, or everyone doing all of them, which is often much funnier.

ALPHABET BLANK

This is a quickie, splendid for older children, and much more difficult than it first appears.

Can you say the alphabet all the way through without saying any of the letters that appear in your full name? For instance, if your name is Katie Pearson, you must say... BCD... FGH... J... LM... Q... UVWXYZ. Once you have got really good at it, try saying it backwards.

Or say it without the letters of the name of your road, or the name of the person you love, or the place that you are travelling to — quite easy if you are travelling to Peru, Ohio or Hull, and quite hard if you are travelling to Lake Cadibarrawirracanna or Llanfihangel-yng-ngwynfa. Or the delightful Icelandic region of Myrdalsjøkull.

TAP TAP TIP TAP

All you need to play this is something that makes a tapping noise. Two pencils knocked together will do, as will a spoon on an empty lunchbox. See what you can find around you. Lightly slapping your own thighs, or those belonging to someone else, will also be fine.

Think of a tune. Try and make it something that everyone should know, not some obscure diddly-oi-doi folk song that you once heard in a Cambridgeshire pub. Then tap out the tune.

It's actually quite hard for those trying to guess, so you may have to do it a few times. If they still don't have a clue, hum the first two notes, and then continue with the tapping. You can increase the number of hummed notes until they get it.

As there are so many tunes in the world, it may help if you narrow down the selection a bit. Good categories include TV theme tunes, nursery rhymes, and Christmas carols.

ALPHABET I-SPY

I-Spy is still an unfailing stand-by for long journeys, especially with small children. But once you have tired of it try this variation.

Take it in turns. The first person names something that they can spy-with-their-little-eye beginning with an A. Next person calls out something beginning with B, next person C, and so it continues. No guessing required, just an ability to look out of the window or around the train carriage, and name something as quickly as possible.

We have a rule that we miss out the letters Q, X and Z, and if you want to be ruthless impose a ten-second time limit to come up with a word, or you are out.

If you go round the alphabet more than once you must take care not to repeat any words.

ANYTHING TO DECLARE, SIR?

This can be played on any form of transport, and is best suited to older children and grown-ups.

One person is the customs officer, and thinks up a rule, which the others must try to work out. So, it might start with the customs official thinking up a simple rule that everything must be red, and declaring, 'I will allow through customs anyone with a pound of tomatoes.'

The next person might declare, 'Well, can I go through customs with some toffees?' (thinking that the rule might be that everything must begin with the letter T), and the customs officer will say, 'No, I'm sorry, sir. I'll have to confiscate them.'

Someone else might try to take a pound of bananas, which will also not be permitted.

Keep taking turns trying to work it out. The customs official may also take another turn, and list something else that he will allow, like a Manchester United shirt. Soon someone will try to take a pair of red socks through, and will be told by the customs official, 'Certainly, sir, have a nice trip!' and everyone will now be trying to find out what a pound of tomatoes, a Man U shirt and a pair of red socks have in common. Once you think you have worked it out, carry on taking a turn so that it helps those who are still guessing. Also, you may think you have it right, only to discover that your next item is disallowed! When everyone has worked it out and been allowed through customs, a new person becomes the official.

'Red' is a pretty easy rule, but they can be much harder. Here are a few examples of other rules:

- It must begin with a vowel: Igloo, Envelope, Aspirin, Octopus, Uneaten sandwich.
- It must have only four letters: bull, lamp, cake, mist, frog.
- It must be round.
- It must be something in the car.
- It must be black and white.
- It must have a double letter: aPPles, buTTer, a trEE, meSSy hair, would all be allowed.

You can think up loads more, and make them less or more difficult, depending on the ability of those playing.

CAN YOU JUST BE QUIET FOR ONE MINUTE!

If you have had enough noise, and find yourself inadvertently shouting the title of this game, read on.

Tell everyone that they must count, in their heads, to sixty seconds, and then call out their name when they think a minute has passed. A timekeeper, meanwhile, keeps an eye on a clock or watch, and makes a note of who was the closest. Everyone can only shout out once in each round. You will find that this restores a little quiet in the back of the car, especially if you award a very small prize for the winner each time.

TOP TIP: If you find one player is constantly winning, check that they don't have a hidden watch or mobile phone with them!

GRANNY CONNIE WENT TO MARKET

Our children seem to have much better powers of memory than we do these days, and that is what is needed in this game. We've named it after our lovely Granny Connie.

The first person starts by saying, 'My Granny Connie went to market and bought a...' Then name anything you fancy, perhaps an elephant. The next person must now say the same thing and then add a new item to the shopping list, say a watering can. So now, the third person must repeat two things and add another. 'Granny Connie went to market and bought an elephant, a watering can and some sharp scissors...' You get the picture. Once you get to the sixth item, it will be getting more and more difficult to remember everything.

If the grown-ups are finding this a little difficult you can make it easier by choosing the list in alphabetical order, the first item beginning with A, the next with B and so on.

Even though the youngest players may need a bit of help when it is their turn to come up with the next item on the shopping list, they can still be invaluable players with their astonishing powers of memory. Be prepared to be defeated by your three-year-old.

HANDS UP!

You can't play this game if you have both hands on the steering wheel, but if you are anywhere else it is always a winner with very young children. Just prepare yourself to have sublime patience, as you will almost certainly tire of the game way before they do.

Find anything small enough to fit into your hand. Put your hands behind your back, decide which hand the object will go in, and wait for your child to give you the order to raise both your clenched fists. If they are old enough to shout 'Hands up!' then great, if not then any old noise will do. When both your fists are in front of them, they must choose which hand is hiding the object. Hands must be tapped to be opened. Be sure to spot the delight in their eyes when they choose the correct hand.

GEOGRAPHY

This is an all-time favourite for those who can spell, but with a bit of prompting, little ones can play too.

Geography is the topic, and you may use names of countries, cities, towns, villages, rivers, mountains, lakes, oceans and even planets.

The first person says the name of any country, e.g. France, and the next person has to say a place starting with the last letter of France, e.g. Egypt. Then the next person has to say a place beginning with the last letter of Egypt, e.g. Tunbridge Wells, and so on. If you are travelling by road, you can keep your eyes peeled for any signs that may help you out.

Needless to say, you are not allowed to repeat any words, nor are you allowed to take too long to come up with an answer (particularly grown-ups).

With younger children, try playing it with different subjects like: girls' names or boys' names, food, football teams, famous people, body parts, cartoon and television characters – whatever they think they know a bit about.

SPOOF

This is a brilliant game for travelling because the only things you need to move are your arms. So even if you are strapped into a car seat, squashed into a minuscule aeroplane seat or being told to sit still with your lifejacket on in a boat, you can still play it. The only things you need to find first are three small objects each, which we shall call 'spoofers', that can easily fit into a clenched fist. Any coins, matchsticks, jelly babies, even small pebbles borrowed from an airport lounge flowerpot will make great spoofers.

All of you put your hands behind your back and fiddle around with your spoofers, secretly deciding how many spoofers to store and hide in your right hand: either all three, two, just one or none at all. You each decide this individually, and you are not allowed to let anyone else know. (It is a good idea if you keep the leftover spoofers tightly hidden in your left hand so that no one can work out how many you have in your right hand.) Then, at the count of three, you all hold your right hand in front of you, keeping your fist tightly shut and palms down so that nobody can see how many spoofers you have decided to hide in it.

The youngest player then starts by guessing, and adding up how many spoofers there are altogether in everybody's right hands. (If there are two of you playing, there could be anything between nought and six spoofers; if there are three of you playing then it will be a number between nought and nine.) Then the player on their left has a turn to guess the total number of spoofers, and so on. Nobody is allowed to say the same number in each round of Spoof. When everyone has guessed, everyone turns their hand over and reveals how many spoofers they were hiding. The one who guessed correctly wins, and is the first person to guess in the next round.

TOP TIP: As you play the game you will soon see that every time someone guesses a number, they may be revealing whether they have got lots of spoofers in their hand or hardly any at all. So pay plenty of attention to the numbers being guessed, and you will soon discover the many ins and outs of tactical Spoof-play.

COUNTDOWN

We vividly remember playing this game as children at the end of almost every car journey we ever went on, however long or short. Don't worry, you don't have to do a Richard Whiteley impression or find Carol Vordeman attractive to play this. You don't even have to know who they are.

When you think you are about two miles from your destination, start counting backwards from one hundred. Count at your own pace and at whichever volume suits the driver. When you get down to 'twelve, eleven, ten' and are still nowhere near arriving, you might have to cheat a bit and start using fractions in order to make the countdown last a bit longer. When you get down to 'five, four and three-quarters, four and a half, four and a quarter' and you are still not there, you have to talk in slow motion, 'Twoooo aaaaand a haaaaalf, twoooo and a quaaaaaaaarteeeeer'...

The aim, of course (aside from annoying the driver), is to get to blast off just as the car is parked and your seatbelts can be undone.

THROWING A SMILE

Some people are really good at this game (like our Dad), and some plainly are not good at it (like Polly, but then she's never really been any good at throwing anything apart from the occasional wobbly. She still loves playing it though).

Someone starts by smiling as much as possible and looking at everyone else, who must keep a straight face despite being demonically leered at. The smiler then raises a hand to their face and covers their mouth, catching the smile in their hand, so that when they take their hand away, they too are straight-faced and solemn. They then throw the smile in their hand at whomever they wish, so the catcher can then beam for a few seconds before they, in turn, throw the smile on to someone else.

We always try and use up all our smiling during our few seconds of being the smiler, but somehow we cannot manage to get the grin off our faces with our hands.

(Maybe if you played this at an airport or a train station other bored spectators would join in if you threw a smile at them.)

OLD MACDONALD

There is no doubt that singing a nursery rhyme that everyone knows can help relieve most fights in the back of a car. However, the sheer boredom of singing 'Old Macdonald had a Farm' over and over again has led to the invention of this game.

Keep using the same tune as 'Old Macdonald', but this time change the words to:

Old Macdonald went to the doc's, E-I-E-I-O,
And he said to the doc,
    I've got a bad cough, E-I-E-I-O.
With a cough, cough here,
    and a cough, cough there,
Here a cough, there a cough,
    everywhere a cough, cough,
Old Macdonald went to the doc's, E-I-E-I-O.

Old Macdonald went to the doc's, E-I-E-I-O,
And he said to the doc,
    I've got itchy spots, E-I-E-I-O.
With a scratch, scratch here,
    and a scratch, scratch there,
Here a scratch, there a scratch,
    everywhere a scratch, scratch,
Old Macdonald went to the doc's, E-I-E-I-O.

The possibilities are endless. If you can't think up

what noise to make for a gammy leg, sore head, clicky bones or rumbling tummy, then just aim to hold on to the sore bit of the body and whimper.

We also did a good one about Old Macdonald going to a monster shop on one journey. In that monster shop he bought a ghost that waved its arms around going 'whooooaa'. He got a spooky laugh that went 'Hoo, hoo, hoo, hahahaha' a bit like Vincent Price. He also bought a pet bat that screeched really badly and a bloodied dagger that went 'Ee-ee-eee-eee' as it went in and out of siblings' tummies. It kept us all amused for miles.

AARDVARKS, AVOCADOS AND ACTION MEN

One of you chooses any object that begins with the letter A, let's say an Action Man. The next person then thinks of a verb beginning with the letter B that you can feasibly do to an action man, let's say 'I Boiled it.' The next person thinks of a verb beginning with C and says 'I Chopped it up,' then 'I Drew on it,' then 'I Examined it,' etc.

You can start anywhere in the alphabet, not just A.

TOP TIP: As we sometimes run out of verbs beginning with Z or X, we either cheat and skip over these letters, or we think of an object starting with a tricky letter and work on from there.

PLASTIC BAG RUSTLE

This game is perfect as an emergency 'stuck-in-a-traffic-jam-all-hell-breaking-loose' kind of game.

There always seems to be an old plastic bag knocking around on the floor of the car. Sometimes it's got rotting apple cores in it, or is hopelessly stuck together with old pay-and-display parking tickets. However, there are times when it's still in a relatively useful state.

Now ask everyone to keep their eyes shut while you place any object you can find, such as a pen, a cassette case, a half-eaten sandwich, a packet of baby wipes, one small sock, even the furry apple core if you wish, into the plastic bag. (We find it works best with one object at a time.) Tie a knot in the top of the bag so that hands cannot get inside it. Then each player must keep their eyes shut whilst they are allowed five seconds to hold the bag and rustle it, trying to guess what is inside. It is a probably a good idea if they don't shout out their answers until everyone has had a go. At the end of five seconds whether they are ready or not they must pass the bag on to the next player. Once everyone has had a feel, the guessing can start. If nobody gets the right answer the bag is passed round again.

Repeat with different items until you make it through the traffic lights.

PAPER AEROPLANES

When was the last time you tried making a paper aeroplane? This is a great thing to do if you are delayed at an airport, have some spare newspaper and think that you've got enough space around you to launch a few missiles.

The basics, if you remember, are as follows. Fold a rectangle in half lengthways and open it out again. Then fold the top two corners into the centre to form triangles. Fold the same corners in exactly the same way again to make long weird triangles, and then again so that your piece of origami is beginning to look really long and thin. Turn it over so the smooth side is facing you and fold in half along the original crease. Then, holding it from underneath so that your top flaps open out as wings, point and launch.

Have races, try and get your plane to hit the coffee-vending machine, or skim over Aunty Jo's head – whatever takes your fancy.

TOP TIP: Do bear in mind that nervous fellow passengers may not wish to hear plane-crashing sounds minutes before they board.

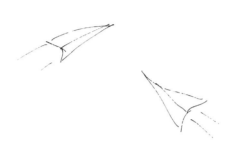

I'M BORED! ...
ON A BEACH

SEAWEED WIGS

Collect up seaweed from along the beach, then drape it on your head for a splendid new look. Try different kinds to see which suits you the best, and remember to shake the seaweed well to dislodge any lurking crabs or unwelcome creepy-crawlies.

For the very brave, you could try some particularly slimy green seaweed (sometimes called sea lettuce) as a rather fetching beard or moustache and eyebrows. Why not ask someone to judge you, and award a bottle of sweet-smelling shampoo as the prize?

FLOTSAM COLLAGES

These are very popular with both children and adults. The only time that it is hard to do them is when the wind is blowing up a real hooley.

Take a wander down the beach and collect up anything that catches your eye: bits of fabric, plastic, rope and string, driftwood and twigs, polystyrene, interesting pebbles, seaweed, palm leaves, coconuts, shoes... anything interesting and colourful that is lying around.

We find that it's best to gather together all your flotsam and then see if an idea leaps out at you. Once we found an old pair of swimming goggles, which we thought could be a pair of glasses, and that gave us the idea to make a girl going to school. She had a very fine multi-coloured school uniform, made from different scraps of coloured material, and bunches in her seaweed and rope hair, and a splendid satchel formed from half a flipper and a salty belt. Her lips were made from bottle tops, her nose from half a tennis ball, and we used pebbles as an outline for good definition. Generally, figures and faces work well, and don't forget to add jewellery, shoes, hats, bags and maybe a parrot on a pirate's shoulder.

If there is nothing on the beach except seaweed and pebbles, they too can make a lovely collage. Use pebbles that are the same colour to create blocks and shapes, and white stones as outlines. You could try a picture of a boat, using pebbles for the boat and seaweed as a churning sea around it.

Other ideas are fishes, sea monsters, mermaids, houses, flowers and animals.

A finished collage or any piece of beach art will look even better if you make a frame for it. Use pebbles, seaweed, drift-wood, or just build a low wall of sand around it. A framed masterpiece is also much more noticeable to passers-by. In North Carolina, where people drive onto the beach in their jeep-loads, a simple picture with an obvious frame was left untouched for days. You could see from the tyre marks that everyone had swerved to avoid it.

MOUSE DINNER PARTIES

Little kids especially love this, and it really gets them using their imaginations.

Lay out a towel or T-shirt as a picnic rug and find some small flat stones as mouse-sized dinner plates. Then look around and see what you could find that might look like food. Here are some pointers to get you started:

• Little shells with a twig sticking out of them might be chicken drumsticks.
• A bit of seaweed could be cabbage or broccoli.
• Can you find some tiny pebbles for roast potatoes?
• Would the mice like tiny boiled eggs in tiny egg cups?
• Can you find something that would do as little cups and saucers?
• What could they have for pudding?
• Do they need knives and forks, or napkins?

You can go on and on inventing all sorts of food depending on what you find on the beach. And, of course, your mouse guests will eat up everything, leaving their plates squeaky clean!

THREE-LEGGED RACE

A classic race which you can make a bit more tricky by using seaweed to tie your ankle to your partner's ankle. If the seaweed breaks you must stop and re-tie it.

Another variation on this game is a five-legged race, with three people tying their ankles together.

TOP TIP: Let the person in the middle decide which leg goes first, and have a packet of crisps ready to soothe any tears from tumbles.

SMALLEST SHELL COMPETITION

Exactly what it sounds like: who can find the smallest shell? This is a hunt for everyone, which can take as long as you like. There is only one rule: the shell must be intact, with no chips or holes.

Also in this category is the heart-shaped stone competition, or the most circular stone, or a stone with a hole in it.

When we play this, the winner gets an extra chocolate Flake in their teatime ice cream.

PEBBLE PANTS

This game does assume that those who wish to play are wearing some sort of pants, knickers or swimming gear. It could also be called sandy pants, but that might lead to an uncomfy journey home at the end of the day.

The name pretty much gives the game away, but there are some variations you could try:

• The most basic form of the game is to see how many pebbles of a roughly similar size you can collect in your pants while standing still.

• Or you can decide on a reasonable number of equal-sized stones and then see who can run the furthest and fastest without any stones dropping out. In this version, you are allowed to use your hands to hold your pants up.

• Lastly, try hopping, jumping, running, star-jumps – anything you fancy – and see how quickly you can make your pebble pants fall down. The use of hands this time is strictly forbidden.

TREASURE HUNTS

Everyone loves these. Treasure hunts can be played in teams or individually, but it's great when the older ones help the little ones a bit. You might need to organise yourself a bit beforehand by writing down lists to hand out, or you can just make it up as you go along, calling out the next object to hunt for as an item is found.

The basic idea is to give each team a number of things to find, and the first one back with all of them, or the team who has found the most items in an agreed time limit, is the winner.

The kind of beach you are on will tend to determine what is reasonable to find, but here's a list that you could choose from: a piece of string, a crab's claw, a bit of red plastic, a feather, three perfectly white pebbles, two perfectly round stones, something with writing on, something that holds water, a piece of fishing line, something that used to be alive, a stick with a v-shaped top, a stone with a hole right through it, something beginning with B, something shiny, something that nobody else has found, something smelly, something yellow, a scrap of blue material, an abandoned shoe, a coconut, something that is still alive (this can include a lost child or granny), something that fell off a boat, just ten grains of sand (much more difficult than it sounds!), a mermaid's purse, a limpet shell, something that floats, something that sinks, a lolly wrapper, an albatross covered in an oil slick... Try to include a mix of the easy and the adventurous!

THE PEBBLE AND DRIFTWOOD RACE

A beach version of an egg and spoon race, using a suitable piece of driftwood or plastic to balance a pebble on. Remember, if you drop your pebble you must go back to the start.

If you want to make this game even more challenging, an impartial onlooker can throw buckets of water at anyone they believe may have an unfair advantage (or who has annoyed them in some trivial way). CAUTION: This added hindrance should only be included on a warmish day, and with a sense of humour.

TOP TIP: The key to winning this is to choose your carrying object carefully and to take it slowly.

UNCLE RALPH'S COMFY CHAIR

You know how hard it can be to get really comfortable on the beach sometimes? If you lie flat on your back, your arms get tired holding your trashy novel and the sun in your eyes makes you squint. If you lie on your front, you get a crick in your neck and sand on your chin and your book is too close to your eyes. Here at last is the solution.

This was first shown to us by a friend in Australia, and it has revolutionised relaxing on the beach for us, particularly when heavily pregnant and extremely ungainly. It's called Uncle Ralph's Comfy Chair because Uncle Ralph loves to relax and hates the word comfy.

Here's what you do. In the place where you would like to sit, face the sea then stand with your legs apart, bend over and dig like a dog with your front paws. Pile up all the sand that comes out of the hole to make a mound behind the hole. Depending on the size of your bottom, the hole should be about eighteen inches deep and wide, and the mound about two feet high. When you have patted it all down firmly and maybe put a sprinkling of warm, dry sand or your towel in the hole, settle down. Your bottom goes in the hole, your back and head rest against the gently sloping mound, and your legs are slightly bent and raised in front of you. Bliss, we promise.

SHADOW DRAWINGS

Try this on a sandy beach, at the end of the day when shadows are getting longer and tempers are getting shorter.

It needs two of you, one to be the model and the other to be the artist. The model strikes a pose that makes an interesting silhouette – maybe arms out to the side, one leg in the air or fingers coming out like antlers on top of your head – then has to stay totally still. The artist then sets to work and quickly traces the outline of the silhouette in the sand.

How about trying to make yourself into each of the letters that spell out your name? (But be prepared for awkward positions, losing your balance and looking as if you are dancing to 'YMCA'.)

BOAT RACES

If you are lucky enough to be on a beach with a stream running through it, you can have a peaceful and serene regatta or fiercely competitive boat races.

Boats can be made from all sorts of things: bits of polystyrene, cork or wood will all bob along nicely. You can decorate them with a twig mast and a paper sail, or a driftwood rudder or a pebble engine. As they float downstream they may encounter obstacles on the way which you can remove, or dig deeper channels if need be. You can also throw stones at them and try to get them to sink.

Experiment with larger boats made from a piece of driftwood, balance pebbles and shells and seaweed on them as their cargo, and see how far they get before you have a major shipping disaster.

Our tremendous Aunt Ros has decided that when she dies she wants her ashes placed on a driftwood boat and sent down a stream and off into the Atlantic on a moonlit night!

STONE TOWERS

A quiet game for those who aren't in the mood for running around. Find some flat, or flattish, stones and pebbles. Start with the larger ones at the bottom and see how high you can make a tower. Balancing as you go along is the key, and you may find that a stone that made the tower wobble too much when further down, is just perfect two stones higher. If you can balance nine, that's pretty impressive.

A series of stone towers in a line along the beach looks fantastic, and if you build them where the tide will come in over them, you can try to guess which one will stay up the longest. The more destructive members of your group can also enjoy throwing stones at them to try to knock them down.

LIMPET NOSE

Limpets are the conical shellfish that live on rocks and are impossible to prise off. However, look along the shore and you will almost certainly find empty shells. If there are no limpets, experiment with other shells.

Find one limpet shell per person. Draw a starting and finishing line in the sand. Balance the limpet shell on your nose by tipping your head back, and then run like crazy. If your limpet falls off your nose (which it probably will), go back to the start. Watch out for stubbed toes in this one — it's hard to look down with your head tipped back.

To play Limpet Eyes, choose two limpet shells each and put them over your eyes instead. There'll be even more stubbed toes with this game, and you might bump into each other as well.

Why not go the whole hog? Put shells on your nose and eyes, and then another balanced on pouting lips.

TOP TIP: Check for hermit crabs before attempting these races!

LONG JUMP

This event is for sandy beaches only; it can be hard on the toes otherwise.

Draw a take-off line and have as long a run-up as you like. Draw a line out to the side to mark where you landed, so that you can judge yourself against the others. For variation try jumping without a run-up, or try jumping backwards.

Be sure to cheer each other along during the run-ups. The winner gets a sandy apple.

DAM IT ALL!

If on your beach you have even a trickle of water, then you need look no further for something for the grown-up men to do. It is a proven sociological fact that fathers find it impossible to sit back and watch a dam being constructed without joining in and bagsying the best spade, ordering everyone else on the beach to keep an eye on one bit of the barrier or other, and sending small children off in search of enormous rocks, which they will dutifully heave back to him before carefully dropping them on their own toes.

Dams are fantastic. Whether you have only sand to pile high to try and hold back the flow to form a lake, or whether you are on a stony beach and become an expert in drystone-walling in order to accomplish a diversion of the water, dams can use up a whole day.

If where you are building your fortification there is a bit of a pong, be aware that you might be damming a sewage outlet. There was often a worried cry from Granny, 'What about the sewage?' whenever we started on our waterworks, but as far as we can remember, we never caught cholera or dysentery.

See if you can divert the stream so that it takes a completely new path, using walls and ditches, or form a big lake by blocking the stream completely. You will need to keep working on this, as the fuller the lake gets, the higher and wider you will have to dam.

HOPSCOTCH

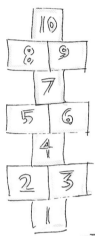

If you have forgotten how to play hopscotch, here's our version. You will need to be on a sandy beach to draw the hopscotch pitch.

A quick recap of the rules: you have to throw your pebble on to each of the numbered squares, starting with the closest, and then hop or jump the length of the pitch and back again without landing on the square that holds your pebble. For example, throw the stone on to square number one, then jump over square one landing on squares two and three, then hop on to four, jump on to five and six, hop on to seven, jump on to eight and nine, then hop on to ten. Then, balancing carefully, turn round on one leg and hopscotch back again, stopping at number two to pick up your pebble, and jump back over number one.

Then throw your pebble on to square two, hop on to square one, hop on to three, hop on to four, jump on to five and six, etc., all the way to ten and back again, stopping at square number three to pick up your stone.

FLIPSTONES, MEET THE FLIPSTONES

Sit down with ten tiny rounded pebbles in front of you. Pick up a stone and place it in the palm of one hand. Throw it up into the air and flip your hand over so that you catch it with the back of your hand. Throw it up again, flipping your hand back once more, catching it in your palm this time. If you have managed to do this without dropping the pebble you can shout 'YABBA-DABBA-DOO'. Now pick up another pebble and try doing the same flips with two stones, then three, then four and so on. You reach official genius status if you can do this with all ten pebbles.

TOP TIP: Keep your fingers firmly together to stop the stones from falling through.

BLINDFOLD RACE

This is one of our favourite races, not least because of the looks you get from other people on the beach – a mixture of admiration, envy and confusion.

Get into pairs – little ones with big ones is obviously the fairest combination. One of you is the runner and the other is the guide. The runner is blindfolded with a T-shirt, sweater or towel, whatever you have to hand, and stands on the starting line.

You can now make the game as difficult as you like. In the simplest version, the guides must stand behind the starting line and shout directions to their runner, instructing them up to a chosen point (maybe a rock, a pile of seaweed or a bucket), round the obstacle and back to where they started. Sounds pretty easy, huh? Just remember there will be other people shouting directions to their runners at the same time, which gets extremely confusing.

Make the race even harder by drawing a course in the sand, and digging holes that must be jumped over.

TOP TIP: Shout encouraging things as well as instructions!

JACKS

This is an excellent game if your energy levels are flagging, and you need some one-handed catching practice.

Take six stones. One stone is for throwing up in the air, and we call this the Jill. Lay out the remaining five stones in front of you. These are your Jacks. Throw the Jill in the air, and with the same hand pick up one of the Jacks before catching the Jill. Then transfer the first jack into your other hand and repeat the process with the other four Jacks.

When you have been successful at picking up the jacks individually, move on to picking them up two by two, then three and two, then four and one, finally picking up all five at the same time before catching the Jill with the same hand.

Apparently, with practice you can get really good at this. Granny Lily is fiendishly good (although she does cheat occasionally). Suzy, on the other hand, is hopeless. Her school reports consistently pointed out how useless she was at throwing and catching, and she hasn't improved in twenty-five years.

SWIMMING ON DRY LAND

If you are on a completely pebbly beach that is very hard to run along, then this is a tremendous race which children find much easier than adults. It leaves you breathless and chortling.

Everyone lies on their stomachs on the pebbles, as if on a starting line. Decide between you where the finishing line is, and at a shout of 'GO!' everyone must propel themselves forward as though they are swimming. It's ridiculously hard work, and the sheer effort of it merits a large chunk of Kit-Kat to the winner.

STONE BOULES

Boys particularly love this game. It becomes quite addictive, and can be played in a wandering fashion, all along the beach and back.

First collect your stones. You need to find one smallish round stone that is easy to spot. Each player then needs to find three larger stones that they can distinguish as their own, either by their markings or by scratching a letter on them with a chalky pebble.

One of the players must throw the small stone, as near or as far as they like, and then everyone takes it in turns to throw one of their own stones, aiming to get it as close to the small stone as possible. Whoever lands one of their stone boules closest to the small stone gets to throw the small stone at the beginning of the next game.

While you all decide who is the winner, it is important to stand around making French noises with your hands on your hips.

PRIZE-WINNING SANDCASTLES

Building sandcastles is still one of the most fun things to do in the world. From a simple mound of sand with one carefully chosen shell on top to an elaborate maze of tunnels, towers and moats, sandcastles are simply one of the finest ways to while away an afternoon.

Here are a few ideas and tips for top creations. Mix and match as you like.

- Dig a trench — square or round or oval, whatever you fancy — but leave a portion of it undug so that you can tunnel underneath it and make a little bridge entrance to your castle. Pile all the sand that you have dug out into the middle to make a good-sized mound which you can then decorate with seaweed, stones, shells, sticks and flotsam.
- When you have forgotten the bucket and spade, or when the sand is too coarse and pebbly to turn into immaculate sandcastles, then make a wonderful Shell Mountain. Simply scoop up a mound with your forearms, the bigger the better, and pat it down firmly. Then decorate every available inch of space with shells or pebbles. The result is surprisingly beautiful. This works really well for smaller children as it does not need any special artistic know-how nor is it at all fiddly.
- Use the edge of a spade to cut in a long flight of

steps up the front of your sandcastle. This instantly adds a palatial feel.

- Make a flag to go on the top from a stick and some seaweed, and find some more greenery to make a garden on the slopes of the mound.
- After making a smooth mound of sand, carve a helter-skelter around the sides, working from top to bottom.

TOP TIP: Watch out for dogs. For some reason, sandcastles are their favourite things to do a wee on, although our dog was always very obliging and only went on other people's sandcastles.

OBSTACLE COURSE

Although you can all do this at the same time, we think there is more fun to be had if an obstacle course is done one by one, with someone timing for the winner. This way, you get to watch everyone else making a fool of themselves too.

A good obstacle course will include as many of the following as you feel like setting up: a trench to jump over (maybe filled with water); a shell to balance on your head or nose; a line to walk along that you mustn't fall off; a pair of shoes to wear that are too big (or too small); a towel to crawl under; a bucket of water to tip over your own head (warm weather only!); a mound to climb over; a line of four stones to balance on top of each other; Granny's hat to put on; specific areas where you must walk like a crab, do a cartwheel, run backwards, do two somersaults, build a sandcastle with your feet, etc.

Be sure to put the course back together again before the next contestant steps up.

EXHIBITION STONES

This is good on any beach with a few stones, shells and a tide line. It's a gentle, contemplative pastime for any age that can use up an hour of cloudy skies.

Find a decent-sized, flat stone not too far from where you have made camp, and brush off any sand and debris. Then hunt around on the beach for anything worthy to display on it: coloured glass with the edges all rounded off (usually known as jewels), perfect shells, a crab's claw, a mermaid's purse, a coconut shell, a bottle top, a feather; anything that you consider good enough to go into the exhibition.

Then arrange your treasure on the chosen exhibition stone and invite people to come and look while you explain what everything is. If it's really good you can charge 5p a visit!

SHIPWRECKED

Choose a good spot in the sand where the tide will come in later on.

Draw the shape of a boat, as if looking at it from above, with its bow pointing towards the sea. Hollow out the sand inside the boat and pile it up to make the sides of the vessel. Then dig a moat around the outside of the boat, again using the displaced sand to pile the sides up even higher.

Once you have the basic structure you can start to add the finer details should you so wish. Build up a seat inside with sand, or use some driftwood and make a steering wheel with a flat stone or bucket. If you can find a couple of long sticks and a beach towel you could make a sail too. More driftwood could make some oars or a rudder.

Then play in your boat and wait for the racing tide to come in and surround you. We like to keep the sides of the boat diligently piled up, getting increasingly hysterical and frantic as the water encroaches, trying to patch holes as they appear, until inevitably our sound ship is water-logged and ship-wrecked.

Other kinds of transport are good too. Try a car (with front and back seats), or even an aeroplane (with rows and rows of seats).

SAND SCULPTURES

These are an alternative to sandcastles for those feeling a little more adventurous. Mould wet sand into shapes and figures to make 3-D pictures. Try making a reclining figure; mermaids work particularly well because you don't have to worry about fiddly below-the-waist bits, and long fish-tails are nice and smooth. You may, however, need to do bosoms, which can be a moment of great merriment. (It's worth betting an ice cream that Dad will think he knows best!)

Once you know how to do mermaid tails, turn anyone who fancies a quick sit-down into a mermaid. Ask them to stretch their legs out in front of them, then cover their legs with sand and add the v-shaped tail just below their feet. If they are still enjoying a sit-down, then start marking out scales on the mermaid's tail.

Other ideas are sea monsters (a good choice if your reclining figure has gone wrong – just add a few more legs and an extra eye or two!), fishes, faces, animals, or a sphinx (that is really quite advanced). If you are not feeling that artistic, then spell out your name or a message in raised letters.

DRIPPY CASTLES

This is a lovely solitary activity, and a good one to cool off a bit. Hot toes can be dabbled in the shallows at the same time.

Sit where the sand is pretty wet and scoop up a handful of sand. Let the sand drip off the ends of your fingers to make a little drippy pile so that it looks a bit like dripping candle wax. When the sand stops dripping easily off your fingertips, discard what is left in your hand, take up another scoop of wet sand and repeat. Soon you will learn the optimum amount of sand and water to form the best drip. Then you can build up any shape of magical castle you choose.

Our sister Emma did this for hours on a Greek beach when she was fourteen and head-over-heels in love with someone whose name she couldn't pronounce. She hoped he would notice her as she sat looking beautiful and dreamy.

FIFTEEN-TO-ONE

This is a game for two players that is best for older children, and people who like to figure puzzles out.

Choose fifteen stones — any size, any shape. Lay them out on the ground in three rows, five stones in each. Taking it in turns, each person takes away one, two, three, four or even five stones, but all must come from the same row.

The person who is forced to pick up the very last stone is the loser, but they get to start the next game.

It sounds a very simple game, but it has you thinking tactically, and the last stages are fiendishly hard to fathom!

SEAWEED TRAP

A game for the more mischievous child.

We're ashamed to say the original seaweed trap, built with our cousin Sophie, in fact contained dead jellyfish. As there don't seem to be so many jellyfish nowadays, and we would not wish to inflict such serious torture on innocent marine life, dead or alive, wet seaweed is an excellent and humane substitute.

Dig a hole in the sand, about one foot deep and wide enough for an unsuspecting adult to stumble into. Fill it with seaweed — really slimy stuff is the best, or that long spaghetti type which gets good and tangled in the victim's toes. When the seaweed is right up to the top of the hole, put a layer of sand over the top to disguise the fact that there is anything amiss.

Now build a street right on top of the pit. Mark it out with pebbles, or sticks, or anything that comes to hand. Then on either side of the street build houses and towers and sandcastles, maybe a stick with some seaweed stuck in the ground for a tree, or see if you can build a church with a steeple. Decorate some of the buildings with shells and stones. The idea is to make it look as if what you have been doing for the last hour or so is simply building a beautiful model village. Then, of course, invite an innocent person to come for a walk down the street... (Maybe don't ask great-granny with her brittle bones.) If it is a success, do a quick bit of repairing and ask another naive member of your party. Uncles are usually a pretty safe bet for a laugh.

SLEEPING SHARKS

Be prepared for high-pitched screams and over-excited youngsters with this one.

This game doesn't have to involve an adult if you really don't fancy getting wet, but the person who is the sleeping shark should be old enough to be able to float around in the shallows without swallowing too much sea water. If you do fancy trying to be the sleeping shark for a few goes, children always seem to get an extra thrill. Maybe they love the idea of lots of kids versus one adult, or maybe it's because, no matter how bad your shark impressions are, you can growl very loudly and scare them pretty easily.

So, decide who is going to be the shark. That person lies down near the shoreline and lets themselves be rolled around by the lapping waves pretending to be asleep. All the other players must approach the shark one at a time, asking, 'Are you awake yet, Mr Shark?' Then with great caution they must try and prod the shark with their finger to see if the shark is indeed awake. The shark is allowed to ignore as many prods as he likes, until he feels it is truly time to wake up. Obviously the prodding has made the shark a little irritable, so he has every right to want to attack the prodders the moment he wakes, in which case he can just pounce and shout and try to catch someone, making as much noise and splash as possible.

Alternatively, he might want to wake up a little more slowly, and prolong the agony of everybody wondering who will be caught. If you are stuck for ideas about what to say, try something along the following lines to get you started. 'Who was it that just woke me up?' 'I've woken up starving hungry, so I'm going to find a nice little fish/girl/boy/aunty to eat.' 'Mmmm! I can smell somebody really close to me. Let me just check my teeth are sharp enough.' Then go for the attack.

TODDLER IN THE HOLE

A winner for a child just learning to stand, or for a toddler who keeps running away.

Dig a hole about as deep as your child's armpits. Then place child in hole (feet downwards!). To keep the little one amused put a few objects like stones (though not ones small enough to be swallowed), shells (likewise), a spade, a lolly stick, a bit of string, a little live crab, whatever you can find, around the hole. If your child is about seven months-old, then all they will want to do is eat enormous handfuls of sand, which makes for very interesting nappies.

AHOY THERE

A good game if you're getting a bit cold and damp and need to have a quick runaround.

Someone is picked as the shark, and everyone else is a sailor. The shark chases all the sailors, and if you are caught you must stand on one leg and call to the other sailors, 'Ahoy there, me hearties, I'm marooned!' or just 'Ahoy there, Ahoy there!' in a rather poor West Country accent. Hopefully someone will come to the rescue. The rescuer must draw a circle in the sand around the marooned sailor's leg. When the circle is complete, both sailors are free to run around again. The rescuer cannot be caught by the shark while he is drawing the circle.

The shark has won when all the sailors are marooned at the same time, and then a new shark is picked for the next game.

We also like to make a little safe island. Dig a hole in the sand, just big enough for one person. This is a place where you can rest if you are getting tired. However, if someone else jumps in, then you must jump

out, no matter how short a time you have been there!
If the shark is finding it too difficult, you can add a
rule that once a sailor has been marooned and
rescued, he is only allowed to hop on one leg.

NOUGHTS AND CROSSES

Find a patch of sandy beach, and draw a noughts-and-
crosses grid in the sand. Then use stones for the
noughts and shells as your crosses.

If you are on a pebbly beach, look for sticks,
seaweed or driftwood to form the grid, and use only
white pebbles perhaps for the crosses, and bits of
found plastic for the noughts.

You may be able to find flat stones on which you
can draw a grid using a chalky stone.

Don't forget to try bumper versions using three-or
four-lined grids, trying to score as many lines of three
as you can.

INDEX

INDEX

NOTE ON THE AUTHORS

Suzy Barratt and Polly Beard are sisters. Suzy lives in Dorset with Joss, Elmo and Lola the dog. Polly lives in London with Tom, Ella and Jojo.

We'd love to know your favourite games or your comments and variations on the games in this book. Please visit our website: www.imboredbooks.com